A HISTORY

OF THE MESILLA VALLEY

1903

AF333219

Maude Elizabeth McFie, May 1903,
as she received her B.A. from
State College, New Mexico.

A HISTORY
OF THE MESILLA VALLEY
1903

by

Maude Elizabeth McFie (Bloom)

edited by

Lansing B. Bloom

annotated by

Jo Tice Bloom

Yucca Tree Press

A HISTORY OF THE MESILLA VALLEY - 1903. Copyright 1998 by Jo Tice Bloom. All rights reserved. No part of this book may be reproduced in any form or by any electronic or mechanical means, including information storage and retrieval systems, without permission, in writing, from the publisher, except by a reviewer who may quote brief passages in a review. Yucca Tree Press, 2130 Hixon Drive, Las Cruces, New Mexico 88005-3305.

First Printing   January 1999

Library of Congress Cataloging in Publication Data.

Bloom, Maude Elizabeth McFie

   A HISTORY OF THE MESILLA VALLEY - 1903
      1. New Mexico, Mesilla Valley - History.   2. New Mexico
        Territory, 1846-1912.
      I. Maude Elizabeth McFie Bloom.   II. Lansing B. Bloom.
       III. Jo Tice Bloom.   IV. Title.

Library of Congress Catalog Card Number: 98-061626

ISBN: 1-881325-33-4

Cover design: Fine Line Design
Cover photo: La Flor del Valle Farm looking west - N. Spatcier, proprietor.
  Courtesy: Rio Grand Historical Collections
        New Mexico State University Library

for Maude's grandchildren

Susan Marie Bloom
John Lansing Bloom
Katherine Elizabeth Bloom Jassen

List of Illustrations

Map

INTRODUCTION

Maude Elizabeth McFie was born April 1, 1880, in Coulterville, Illinois, the second child and first daughter of Mary B. Steel McFie and John Robert McFie, married in 1876. The first child, Ralph, was born in 1877. Maude was followed by twins, Mary and John, born in 1889, and the youngest child, Amelia, born in 1893. The three younger children were all born in Las Cruces or Mesilla.

Mary Barr Steel, born on December 10, 1852, was of Scotch-Irish descent. Her family had come to the United States in 1848 and settled in St. Louis, eventually moving to Coulterville, Illinois. Her three sisters, Annie, Eliza and Maggie, also migrated to the Las Cruces-Mesilla world in the years immediately following the McFies' move. Eventually their widowed mother joined them. They were loyal members of the Presbyterian Church and active in many groups in south central New Mexico. Mary's sister Annie married first cousin Samuel A. Steel, a widower who owned the Mesilla Valley Dairy. Eliza married John Richard DeMier, who was active in several occupations. They lived in Alamogordo and Santa Fé as well as Las Cruces. The youngest sister Maggie married the Rev. John Riley Cooper. Mary Steel McFie, Maude's mother, was instrumental in founding the Women's Improvement Association in Las Cruces, was an active member of the Women's Club of Santa Fé, and of other civic organizations. She was remembered for her volunteer work and contributions to community life.

John R. McFie was born in Washington County, Illinois, on October 9, 1848, the son of Scottish immigrants. He grew up on the family farm in Randolph County, attending local schools. At age sixteen, in February 1864, he joined the Thirtieth Illinois Veteran Volunteer

John R. McFie

Infantry and marched to the sea in Georgia under the command of General William T. Sherman. Following the war, McFie returned to Illinois, clerked in a dry goods store in Coulterville and then read law in Sparta. During the thirteen years he practiced law in Chester, he also served in the Illinois state legislature. He was a loyal Republican. Through the intervention of General John L. Logan and other Republicans, McFie was appointed Register of the U.S. Land Office in Mesilla in 1884, taking up his official work on March 14th. His wife and two children, Ralph and Maude, joined him in May.

In 1885, John McFie began practicing law in Las Cruces and riding the court circuit with Col. A. J. Fountain, Thomas B. Catron, Stephen B. Elkins, Albert Fall, and other lawyers who had immigrated to New Mexico. With the small population and wide open spaces, most men active in politics, the law, and business knew each other and worked together, sometimes for common goals and sometimes not. He was instrumental in the chartering of the College of Agriculture and Mechanic Arts (now New Mexico State University) in 1888—along with his brothers-in-law Samuel A. Steel and John R. DeMeir—and served as President of the first Board of Regents. McFie was first appointed to the Territorial Supreme Court as Associate Justice in 1889, serving the four years of his commission. His appointment was not renewed by a Democratic president, Grover Cleveland. Reappointed to the court (the Santa Fé district) in 1898 by President William McKinley, he held that position until statehood in 1912. The family moved to Santa Fé in 1898, where Judge McFie was active in the First Presbyterian Church, the Grand Army of the Republic, the Santa Fé Archaeological Society and other community activities. He was a founder of the Museum of New Mexico and the School of American Research located in Santa Fé.[1]

Ralph and Maude grew up in Mesilla and Las Cruces, receiving their early education in the local schools, including the college preparatory school. They were both fluent in Spanish and English as a result of the bicultural environment of the area and their parents' interests. Both Ralph and Maude went to the A. and M. College in Las Cruces. A cousin, Samuel Steel, had been in the first class at the 'Aggie' school, but was murdered before he could graduate. During his student years, Ralph served as his father's driver when his father

above: McFie Hall, State College, New Mexico.
below: Basketball team from State College. *l. to r.:* Bonnie
McLaughlin, Beth ??, Vinette Davis, Maisie Sebben, Maude McFie

followed the court circuit. Watching and listening to the cases, Ralph developed his own 'Spanish shorthand' which stood him in good stead for many years. In 1898 he moved with the family to Santa Fé and began to read law, planning to follow in his father's footsteps. When war against Spain was declared in 1898, he joined the Rough Riders. During the invasion of Cuba, he gained the attention of Col. Theodore Roosevelt through his knowledge of Spanish. In 1901 he was appointed secretary to William Howard, Governor of the Philippines, and moved to the Philippines where he spent the rest of his life as a government administrator, a judge and the owner of several plantations on the island of Mindanao. He died in 1930, leaving a widow and a daughter.[2]

John R. McFie, Jr., and his twin sister Mary, attended the preparatory school and the College. Later they transferred to the University of Michigan where John was active in extracurricular activities. Following his graduation from the University of Michigan Law School in 1914, he was admitted to the bar in New Mexico and practiced law in Santa Fé, Gallup, and Albuquerque, often in partnership with his father. He was appointed a regent of the University of New Mexico. He served in the infantry during World War I. By 1922 he had joined his brother, Ralph, in the Philippines, where he practiced law in Manila and had many business interests. Following the Japanese invasion in 1942, he and his wife were interned at Santo Tomás University. He was killed by shell fragments in February 1945, as the United States was liberating the Philippines, leaving his widow and two stepsons.[3]

Mary studied at the University of Michigan and received her bachelor's degree from the Bush Conservatory of Music in Chicago, later earning a master's degree from the University of New Mexico. Throughout her life she taught music in the public schools, especially in Santa Fé and Belen, and directed choirs in both towns. She married Lawrence Lackey, a graduate of the University of New Mexico and a salesman for the Charles Ilfeld Company. During her marriage and following her divorce, she made her home in Santa Fé, Albuquerque, and Belen. She had two daughters and son. At her death in 1980 she was living in Long Beach, California.

above: The Las Cruces McFie home built c. 1889. Judge and Mrs. McFie are on the porch, Ralph at top of stairs, and Maude on Ralph's buckskin pony. *below:* The double drawing rooms of the McFie home. They moved in the year the twins were born. The Knabe piano was purchased from Mr. Dessaur who had it freighted from St. Louis.

The youngest McFie, Amelia, grew up in Santa Fé and graduated from the University of New Mexico. In 1926 she became one of the original couriers for Fred Harvey's Indian Detours. Drawing on her family and personal knowledge of Indians and New Mexico, she guided tourists throughout the Fred Harvey-Santa Fe Railroad southwestern empire. When the depression of the 1930s decreased the Indian Detours business, Amelia joined the Santa Fe Railroad as a travel agent, becoming one of the first women to serve aboard Santa Fe trains. Eventually she retired and married Warren S. Thompson and they set up a home in Grass Valley, California. She died in 1982 at the home of a niece in California.

Maude attended the A & M College, as well as the preparatory school. Mrs. McFie maintained a home in Las Cruces while the children attended the preparatory school and the college. In college, Maude played basketball for three years, served on the staff of the literary magazine and the yearbook for four years, went on outings at Dripping Springs and led a rather typical coed life for her time. She majored in history. Like all seniors at the College, she was required to present a senior thesis as a requirement for graduation. Her thesis was supervised and signed by Prof. Hiram Hadley of the History Department.

In writing her history of the Mesilla Valley, Maude had two great advantages that many college seniors do not have—her parents knew almost everyone of importance in Las Cruces, Doña Ana County and southern New Mexico as well as many people in the northern part of the territory. Maude was able to interview pioneers such as Samuel G. Bean and Pablo Melendrez [junior]. She knew A. J. Fountain and Pat Garrett. For her, history was very much alive. Thus, her thesis has become almost a primary source. She quotes men and their letters which are no longer extant. She knew the landscape. Her thesis has withstood the years in presenting a first-hand knowledge of the Mesilla Valley.

In 1903, Lansing B. Bloom arrived in Las Cruces as a 'lunger.' Born in Auburn, New York, on April 12, 1880, Lansing descended from many generations of middle class New Englanders. He graduated from Williams College in 1902, later earning a master's degree from the Massachusetts college in 1912. He planned to become a

above: During their trip to Geneva, Switzerland, Maude (*left*), Mr. and Mrs. Numa Reymond take a boat to see the Fété des Narcissus.

left: The McFie Children: *seated l. to r.:* Ralph Elmo (18) Amelia May (2½), Maude Elizabeth (15); *standing l. to r.:* twins John Robert, Jr. and Mary Isabelle (7). April 1896.

Maude Elizabeth McFie Bloom wedding photo.
1907

Lansing Bartlett Bloom wedding photo.
1907

Presbyterian minister, and was ordained at the Auburn Theological Seminary in 1907. Tuberculosis was almost epidemic in the eastern United States at this time, so it was not surprising that he contracted the lung disease. Lansing joined innumerable other men and women who traveled to New Mexico and recovered their health. Most of them stayed and helped to found a new state and develop its potential. Lansing Bloom helped to write its history.

At the First Presbyterian Church in Las Cruces, on a Sunday evening in 1903, he met Maude McFie. The obvious happened, to the disappointment of the McFies. They were not excited about the prospect of a minister for a son-in-law. In a parental effort to separate the two, Maude went to Geneva, Switzerland, as an English instructor for six months. Upon her return, she was appointed an instructor in vocal music at the college and joined her mother and younger siblings in their home in Mesilla Park. Later she attended the University of Michigan, while chaperoning the twins, Mary and John, who were also students at the university. The best laid plans of parents are not always successful, and Maude and Lansing were married in Santa Fé in 1907. They left immediately for his first missionary assignment in Saltillo, Mexico.

In the years that followed, Maude wrote history and fiction while Lansing followed his missionary call at Jemez Pueblo and Magdalena, New Mexico. In 1915 they moved to Santa Fé where he became an employee of the Historical Society of New Mexico which operated the Museum of New Mexico. He also worked for the School of American Research. She bore four children during these years; the oldest daughter and son died as babies. Lansing was appointed first co-editor of the *New Mexico Historical Review* when the Historical Society began publishing it. In 1929 he was appointed assistant professor of history at the University of New Mexico. The family, now including daughter Carol and son John, moved to Albuquerque, where Maude and Lansing spent the rest of their lives.[4]

She was very active in the Republican Women's Club, in the Women's Club of Santa Fe, the Presbyterian Church, and other civic groups. She continued these activities when they moved to Albuquerque. She also published several historical essays in the *New Mexico Historical Review*, and some fiction in *McLean's Magazine*. Her play

"Tonita of the Holy Faith" was performed at the 1924 Santa Fé Fiesta and published by the School of American Research.[5] When Lansing made research trips to Mexico City, Spain and Italy, Maude went along as his translator and interpreter. Although he spoke, read and wrote Spanish easily, Maude had grown up bilingual in Las Cruces and helped to screen material for microfilming and translation.

Lansing Bloom died in Albuquerque on February 14, 1946. His widow continued to live in the family home into her eighties. Eventually she moved to Washington, D.C., to be near her son John Porter Bloom. She died on February 14, 1973, in northern Virginia. They are both buried in the family plot in Fairview Cemetery in Santa Fé. She was a historian, a writer, a mother, a wife, a helpmate, and a significant person in the history of New Mexico.

This edition of McFie's thesis is based on the carbon copy manuscript in the possession of her son, John Porter Bloom, of Las Cruces, New Mexico. The original thesis is in the Special Collections of New Mexico State University Library. Maude did her research and writing in the spring of 1903, conducting many oral history interviews. That spring Maude and her cousin, Professor John Oliver Miller of the College commercial department, drove throughout Doña Ana County talking with old timers and old friends. While she talked Cousin John took shorthand notes. She and Lansing planned to update, expand, and publish the thesis.[6] The carbon copy manuscript shows the work of both Maude and Lansing as they began to prepare the manuscript for publication. Lansing's pencil comments are interlined and in the margins of the manuscript. Using his emendations, the current editor, Jo Tice Bloom, has incorporated his suggestions into the body of the thesis. The 1903 writing syle was much more verbose and flowery than that of the present, but the author's style has not been changed or modified for readers in the 1990s. The editor has added initials or full names (where possible) and corrected obvious typographical errors. Otherwise the History is as Maude wrote it in 1903, including her chapter and section divisions and headings. In some cases her notes have provided material for additional footnotes and these are indicated by 'M.E.M.' Notes added by Lansing Bloom are identified by 'L.L.B.' Jo Tice Bloom has corrected inaccurate quotations and updated the footnote format, as well as correcting footnotes and a few dates, as indicated by 'J.T.B.'

Prof. Lansing B. Bloom, Maude E. Bloom, Carol Lansing (12), and John Porter (3½) at a hotel in Seville, Spain, in 1928. The hotel was on Calle Santa Ana.

Citation of works consulted and used for information was different in 1903. The current editor has worked to make citations as accurate as possible. Maude McFie, as author, had a tendency to adapt quotations to her style of writing. These adaptations, usually limited to punctuation and underlining, have been corrected and all quotations have been edited to conform with the originals. The editor has added endnotes according to standards of 1998. The endnotes are based on Maude's sources and every effort has been made to provide correct quotations and sources. Information on many people mentioned in the text has been added to help in identifying historic individuals. References to more recent works on various subjects have also been added.

Special thanks go to Cheryl Wilson and John P. Wilson for the excellent help and advice they provided in searching out sources material. Mary Lucille Lackey Foreman and Mary Rhoda McFie Davidson provided family history and photographs. Editor Janie Matson has provided invaluable advice. The editor is deeply grateful to John Porter Bloom for the opportunity to annotate and edit this manuscript and for his unqualified support of this project.

Jo Tice Bloom
October 1998
Las Cruces, New Mexico

Notes:

[1] A short biography of John R. McFie can be found in *New Mexico Historical Review*, V: 411-418 (October 1930).

[2] For a dramatic account of Ralph McFie's life, see Maude McFie Bloom, "Ralph Elmo McFie: From Las Cruces to Davao," *New Mexico Historical Review*, XVII: 64-86 (January 1942).

[3] *New Mexico Historical Review*, XX: 184-186 (April 1945); and Eva Jane Matson, *It Tolled for New Mexico* (Las Cruces: Yucca Tree Press, 1994), pp. 14, 412.

[4] On Lansing B. Bloom see Paul A.F. Walter, "Lansing Bartlett Bloom"; Edgar L. Hewett, "Lansing Bartlett Bloom"; France V. Scholes, "Research Activities of Lansing B. Bloom in Foreign Archives"; "Epilogue of Lansing Bartlett Bloom"; "Bibliography of Lansing Bartlett Bloom"; and "Phi Alpha Theta Testimonial" all in *New Mexico Historical Review*, XXI: 93-119 (April 1946).

[5] Edgar L. Hewett, "Plan of the Fiesta," *Art and Archaeology*, VIII: 203, 205 (December 1924); and Paul A.F. Walter, "The Santa Fe Fiesta of September, 1924," *Art and Archaeology*, XVIII: pp. 189-190. Also Maude McFie Bloom, "Tonita of the Holy Faith," *Papers of the School of American Research*, Santa Fé, 1924.

[6] See "Epilogue of Lansing Bartlett Bloom," *New Mexico Historical Review*, XXI: 111 (April 1946).

A

THESIS

<u>A HISTORY OF MESILLA VALLEY</u>

Submitted by

MAUDE ELIZABETH McFIE

to

THE REGENTS AND FACULTY

of the

<u>NEW MEXICO COLLEGE OF AGRICULTURE AND MECHANIC ARTS</u>

Mesilla Park, New Mexico

June, 1903

TABLE OF CONTENTS

CHAPTER I

CHAPTER II

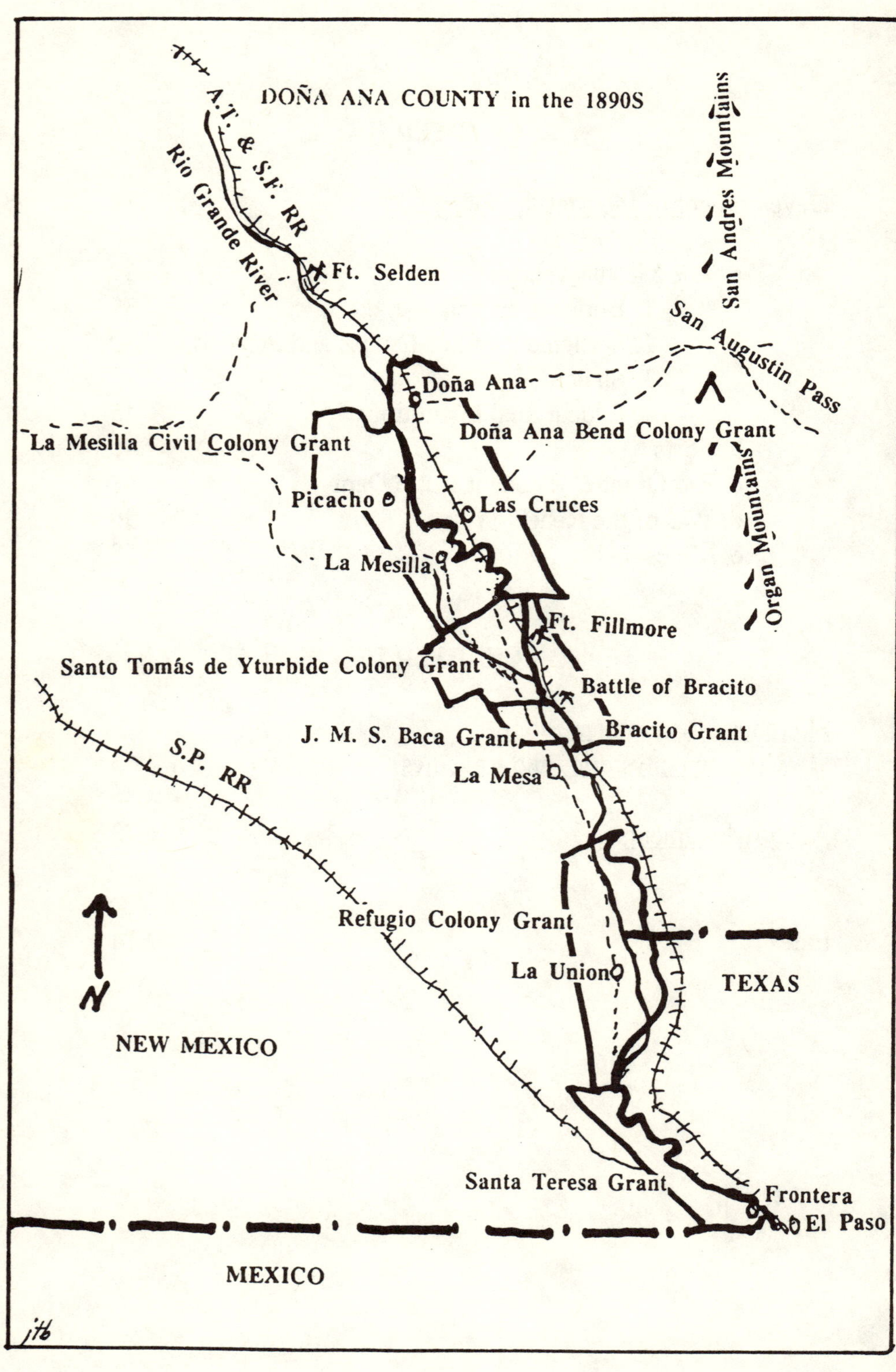

DOÑA ANA COUNTY in the 1890S
A.T. & S.F. RR
Rio Grande River
San Andres Mountains
San Augustin Pass
Ft. Selden
Doña Ana
La Mesilla Civil Colony Grant
Doña Ana Bend Colony Grant
Picacho
Las Cruces
Organ Mountains
La Mesilla
Ft. Fillmore
Santo Tomás de Yturbide Colony Grant
Battle of Bracito
J. M. S. Baca Grant
Bracito Grant
La Mesa
S.P. RR
Refugio Colony Grant
N
La Union
TEXAS
NEW MEXICO
Santa Teresa Grant
Frontera
El Paso
MEXICO

A HISTORY OF MESILLA VALLEY

by
Maude Elizabeth McFie (Bloom)
June 1903

Chapter I

History of South Western United States
Previous to United States Rule

"Before Plymouth Rock had a name, the Spaniards had reached the Rockies," but very meager, indeed, is the information relating to our beautiful little Mesilla Valley for the period during which Spain ruled this vast territory. Mexico, or New Spain, was one of the four Viceroyalties of the Spanish colonies in America, the first Viceroy of Mexico having been appointed in 1538. In 1560 an *Audiencia* was established in Mexico, dividing the country into two *audiencial* districts; New Mexico remained under the jurisdiction of the one at the City of Mexico. During the Spanish period only two grants of land were made which bear directly on this valley: that called Santa Teresa in the year 1768, and the Bracito Grant made in 1818.[1]

When the country passed from Spanish to Mexican possession, great areas were portioned off into grants, such that 224,000 acres in the Mesilla Valley were confirmed in only six grants.

In January, 1824, a General Constituent Congress convened and on January 31st, this body issued a decree to the effect that the Mexican nation consisted of the provinces which formerly constituted the

Viceroyalty of New Spain. States of the new Federation were created consisting of sections of the country, and our Mesilla Valley lay in the "Internal State of the North," the whole of which included the Provinces of Chihuahua, Durango and New Mexico. This was the status of New Mexico only until July 6th of that same year, when it was made a Territory of the nation, and so continued until it became a Department, on December 20th, 1836. The El Paso District was made part of the state of Chihuahua.

The Constitution of 1824 did not prescribe any form of government for territories, and there appears [to be] no law directly on the subject, but numerous laws, at a subsequent date, recognize the existence in these territories of governors and Territorial Deputations.

The Mesilla Valley was then a beautiful mass of vegetation, traversed constantly by all who went and came between Santa Fé to the north and the other provinces, or States, to the south. The earliest settlement in the valley of which I have accurate information, is that of a ranch owned by Don Juan Antonio García, located upon what is now called the Bracito Grant, for he was the original founder of that grant. Pablo Melenudo [Melendrez], who has been dead many years, was, together with his father, employed as a herder upon the ranch in 1822; in the summer of which year all the occupants were driven off by the Indians.

Also, on fairly good authority—though I will by no means state the below is absolutely true—a man by the name of Antonio Buenavides had a wooden house at Cañoncito, a small place down the valley between 15 and 18 miles above El Paso, and had made an irrigation ditch, in 1813 or thereabouts.

In 1841 when the prisoners of the Texan Santa Fé expedition were taken south through this valley, Mr. Kendall, author of "Kendall's Expedition," was one of them, and he states definitely that there was no settlement between the villages of Socorro and El Paso.[2]

The next inhabitants came in the spring of 1842, under the seal of the Mexican government, to an *ancon*, or bend, in the Rio Bravo del Norte, the river now called the Rio Grande. This was the foundation of the town of Doña Ana and will be treated of later under the subject of 'grants.'

The war with Mexico was over the boundary line which Texas

claimed when she entered the Union, namely, that her western boundary was the Rio Grande from its mouth to its source, and then a line due north to 42°. Mexico maintained that the Nueces River was the boundary. A U.S. army under Gen. Zachary Taylor occupied the disputed territory in January, 1846 and hostilities were quickly begun.

The aggressive was taken by Mexico, and the United States made an immediate and spirited reply, war being formally declared on May 13, 1846.

August 18th, 1846, saw the United States flag unfurled over Santa Fé and the Department of New Mexico by Gen. [Stephen W.] Kearny. A portion of the 'Army of the West,' consisting of nearly one thousand brave Missouri volunteers and commanded by Col. Alexander F. Doniphan, passed down the river, having for its goal, Chihuahua; but its near approach frightened away the Mexican troops under Gen. [José Manuel] Monterde at Doña Ana.[3] The Mexican troops under Gen. Monterde marched as far north as Doña Ana to oppose them, but retreated southwards before the appearance of the American force.

On December 14th, Col. Doniphan dispatched Maj. [William J.] Gilpin over the "Jornada del Muerto," that notoriously fearful sandy waste of ninety miles lying northeast of us, with three hundred men; on the 16th he started an additional force of two hundred, and, on the 19th he himself marched down with the remainder of his command, including the provisions and part of the baggage trains. The following has been taken verbatim from Doniphan's Expedition written by J.T. Hughes, of the Regular Missouri Cavalry, who is considered the best authority:

On the 22nd of December, Col. Doniphan overtook the detachment under Lieut. Col. Jackson and Maj. Gilpin near the little Mexican town, Dona Ana. Here the soldiers found plenty of grain, and other forage for their animals, running streams of water, and an abundance of dried fruit, corn meal, and sheep and cattle. These they purchased; therefore, they soon forgot the sufferings and privations which they experienced on the desert. Here they feasted and reposed.

The army now encamped with in the boundaries of the State of Chihuahua. The advanced detachments under Lieut. Col. Jackson and Major Gilpin, apprehending an attack from the Mexicans about the 20th, had sent an express to Col. Doniphan, then on the desert, requesting him to quicken his march. Capt. Reid, with his company, had proceeded about twelve miles below Dona Ana for the purpose of making a reconnaissance, and of acting as a scout or advance guard. While encamped in the outskirts of a forest on a point of hills which command the Chihuahua road, on the night of the 23rd one of his sentinels hailed the Mexican spies in the Spanish language. The spies, mistaking the sentinel for a friend, advanced very near. At length, discovering their mistake, they wheeled to effect their escape by flight. The sentinel leveled his rifle-yager, and discharged the ball through the bodies of two of them.[4] One of them tumbled from his horse, dead, after running a few hundred yards, and the other at a greater distance. Their dead bodies were afterwards discovered. The sentinel was Frank Smith of Saline.

On the morning of the 24th, the whole command, including Lieut. Col. Mitchell's escort, and the entire merchant, provision, and baggage trains, moved off in the direction of El Paso, and, after progress of 15 miles, encamped on the river for water. The forage was only moderately good, therefore the animals, which were not tethered, rambled and straggled far off into the adjacent thickets during the night. The weather was pleasant.

On the morning of the 25th of December, a brilliant sun, rising above the Organ Mountains to the eastward, burst forth upon the world in all it's effulgence. The little army, at this time not exceeding 800 strong was comfortably encamped on the east bank of the Del Norte. The men felt frolicsome indeed. They sang the cheering Yankee Doodle and Hail Columbia. Many guns were fired in honor of Christmas Day. But there was no need of all this, had they known the sequel.

At an early hour the colonel took up the line of march, with a strong front and rear-guard. The rear-guard, under Capt. Moss, was delayed for a considerable part of the day in bringing up the trains, and the loose animals which had rambled off during the night. A great number of men were also straggling about in search of their lost stock. These were also delayed.

While on the march the men most earnestly desired that, if they had to encounter the enemy at all, they might meet him this day. They were gratified; for, having proceeded about 18 miles, the colonel pitched his camp at a place called Brazito, or the Little Arm, on the east bank of the river, in an open, level, bottom prairie, bordered next the mountains and river on the east and southeast by mezquite and willow chaparral. Here the front guard had called a halt.

While the men were scattered everywhere in quest of wood and water for cooking purposes, and fresh grass for their animals, and while the trains and straggling men were scattered along the road for miles in the rear, a cloud of dust, greater than usual, was observed in the direction of El Paso, and in less than 15 minutes some of the advance guard coming at full speed, announced to the colonel, "that the enemy was advancing upon him."[5]

The bugler was summoned. Assembly call was blown. The men, dashing down their loads of wood and buckets of water, came running from all quarters, seized their arms, and fell into line under whatever flag was most convenient. As fast as those in the rear came up, they also fell into line under the nearest standards. The officers dashed from post to post, and in an incredibly short space of time the Missourians were marshaled on the field of fight.

By this time the Mexican general had drawn up his forces in front, and on the right and left flank of Col. Doniphan's lines. Their strength was about 1300 men, consisting of 514 regular dragoons, an old well known corps from Vera Cruz and Zacatecas, and 800 volunteers, cavalry and infantry, from El Paso and Chihuahua, and 4 pieces of artillery. They exhibited a most gallant and imposing appearance; for the dragoons were dressed in a uniform of blue pantaloons, green coats trimmed with scarlet, and tall caps plated in front with brass, on the tops of which fantastically waved plumes of horse hair, or buffalo's tail. Their bright lances and swords glittered in the sheen of the sun. Thus marshaled, they paused for a minute.

Meanwhile, Col. Doniphan and his field and company officers, appeared as calm and collected as when on drill, and in the most spirited manner encouraged their men by the memory of their forefathers, by the past history of their country, by the recollection of the Battle of Okeechobee, which was fought on the same day in 1837, and by every consideration which renders life, liberty and country valuable, to cherish no other thought than that of victory.

Before the battle commenced, and while the two armies stood marshaled front to front, the Mexican commander, Gen. Poncé de Leon, dispatched a lieutenant to Col. Doniphan bearing a black flag. This messenger, coming with the speed of lightening, halted when within 60 yards of the American lines, and waved his ensign gracefully in salutation. Hereupon, Col. Doniphan, advancing towards him a little way, sent his interpreter, T. Caldwell, to know his demands. The ambassador said: "The Mexican general summons your commander to appear before him." The interpreter replied: "If your General desires peace, let him come here." The other rejoined: "Then we will break your ranks and take him there." "Come then and take him," retorted the interpreter. "Curses be upon you, prepare for a charge, we neither ask nor give quarter," said the messenger, and waving his black flag over his head, galloped back to the Mexican lines.

At the sound of the trumpet the Vera Cruz dragoons, who occupied the right of the enemy's line of battle, first made a bold charge upon the American left. When within a few rods the yagermen opened a most deadly fire upon them, producing great execution. At the same crisis, Capt. Reid with a party of 16 mounted men (for the rest were all on foot) charged upon them, broke through their ranks, hewed them to pieces with their sabers, and there by contributed materially in throwing the enemy's right wing into confusion. A squad or section of dragoons, having flanked our left, now charged upon the commissary and baggage trains, but the gallant wagoners opened upon them a well-directed fire, which threw them into disorder, and caused three of their number to pay the forfeit of their lives.

The Chihuahua infantry and cavalry were posted on their left, and consequently operated against our right wing. They advanced within gunshot, and took shelter in the chaparral, discharging three full rounds upon our lines before we returned fire. At this crisis Col. Doniphan ordered the men to "lie down on their faces, and reserve fire until the Mexicans came within 60 paces." This was done. The Mexicans supposing they had wrought fearful execution in our ranks, as some were falling down, while others stood up, began now to advance, and exultingly cry, "Bueno, bueno," whereupon our whole right wing suddenly rising up, let fly such a galling volley of yager balls into their ranks that they wheeled about and fled in the utmost confusion.

By this time the Howard company and others occupying the centre had repulsed the enemy with considerable loss, and taken possession of one piece of his artillery, and the corresponding ammunition. This was a brass 6-pound howitzer. Sergeant Calaway, and a few others of that company first gained possession of this piece of cannon, cut the dead animals loose from it, and were preparing to turn it upon the enemy, when Lieut. Kribben, with a file of artillerymen, was ordered to man it.

The consternation now became general among the ranks of the Mexicans, and they commenced a precipitate retreat along the base of the mountains. Many of them took refuge in the craggy fastnesses. They were pursued by the Americans about 1 mile; Capt. Reid and Capt. Walten, who by this time had mounted a few of his men, followed them still further. All now returned to camp and congratulated one another on the achievement. The Mexican loss was 71 killed, 5 prisoners, and not less than 150 wounded, among whom was their commanding officer, Gen. Poncé de Leon. Also a considerable amount of ammunition, baggage, wine, provisions, blankets, guns, and several stands of colors were among the spoils. A number of horses were killed, and several were captured. The Americans had eight men wounded, none killed.

In this engagement, Col. Doniphan, his officers, and men displayed the utmost courage and determined resolution to conquer or perish in the conflict. Defeat would have been ruinous. Therefore, all the companies vied with each other in endeavoring to render the country the most important service. The victory was complete on the part of the Americans. The battle continued about 30 minutes, and was fought about 3 o'clock p. m., on Christmas Day, at Brazito, 25 miles from El Paso.

Not more than 500 of Col. Doniphan's men were present when the battle commenced. The rest fell in line as they were able to reach the scene of battle. Those who had been far in the rear during the day when they heard the firing came running in haste with their arms in their hands, to bring aid to their comrades, who were then engaged with the enemy. This created such a dust that the enemy supposed a strong reinforcement was marching to our support. This circumstance, also contributed to strike terror into the Mexican ranks.

By this defeat, the Mexican army was completely disorganized and dispersed. The volunteer troops returned with the utmost expedition to their respective homes, while the regular troops continued their flight to Chihuahua, scarcely halting for refreshments in El Paso. On their retreat many of the wounded died. Several were found dead by the road side and the chaparral near the battle field was stained with the blood of the retreating foe. The field was all trophied over with the spoils of the slain and the vanquished. Martial accouterments, sacks and wallets of provisions, and gourds of the delicious wines of El Paso were profusely scattered over miles of surface. These supplied our soldiers with a Christmas banquet. The whole affair resembled a Christmas frolic. This night the men encamped on the same spot where they were when attacked by the Mexicans. Having eaten the bread and drunk the wine which were taken in the engagement, they reposed on their arms, protected by a strong guard.

On the following morning the dead were buried, and the wounded Mexican prisoners comfortably provided with means of conveyance to El Paso. Every needful attention was also given our own wounded by the surgeons. The column, now in perfect order, with the baggage, provision, hospital, ammunition, and merchant trains in the rear, and a strong rear and front guard and a party of flankers on the right and left, moved cautiously in the direction of El Paso, apprehending another attack. After an advance of 15 miles, camp was selected near a small salt lake, where there was a moderate supply of natural forage, such as grass and rushes. From this point Col. Doniphan sent back an express for the artillery to hasten forward, for he anticipated strenuous opposition at El Paso.

While encamped here, one of the picket guard, discovering a party of Mexicans passing along the base of the mountains towards the east, in which they had taken shelter during the day, endeavoring to make good their retreat to El Paso, under cover of night, fired on them. This produced an alarm in camp. The men were cooking their suppers, some of them had spread their beds for repose. Col. Doniphan ordered the fires to be extinguished. Whatever was in the vessels on the fire cooking was now turned topsy-turvy in the effort to put out the light. For a moment all was confusion. Quickly, however, Col. Doniphan drew up his men in lines of battle and awaited the approach of the enemy. Lieut. Col. Jackson in the hurry to parade his men, mounted his mule bare-back, with his sword and shot gun. Many of the men were in ranks barefooted and only half-clad; for they had been roused from slumber. Finally no enemy appearing, the soldiers were ordered to repair to their tents and sleep on their arms. They ran, leaping and hallooing and cursing the false alarm. Before day another false alarm called them out in a similar manner. Therefore, this night the soldiers were much vexed.

The same order of march which had been adopted on the previous day was continued on the 27th, until the column reached El Paso. On arriving at the Great Pass, or gorge in the mountains, through which the river appears to have forced its way, debauching into the valley below, over a system of rocky falls, in dashing cataracts, the colonel was met by a deputation of citizens from El Paso, bearing a white flag, proposing terms of peace, and offering to surrender the place into his hands, beseeching at the same time that he would use his clemency towards them in sparing their lives and protecting their property. This the colonel was inclined to do. It was now about 6 miles to the city. All moved on, rejoicing in the prospect of rest, and something to appease the appetite.

Thus on the 27th, the city of El Paso was possessed by the American troops without further opposition or great effusion of blood. It was night now. There the soldiers camped and enjoyed the advantage of a little repose.[6]

Hon. S[amuel] G. Bean, of Las Cruces, was in Doniphan's army and was engaged in this battle.

This Mexican war resulted in two noted treaties.

On February 2nd, 1848, at a little place called Hidalgo, near the City of Mexico, took place the signing of the treaty called the Guadalupe-Hidalgo treaty by which Mexico gave up 522,568 square miles of land and received $15,000,000. Furthermore, the United States guaranteed to pay claims of our citizens against Mexico to the amount of $3,500,000. This vast territory included not only the present California, New Mexico, Nevada, Arizona and Utah, but parts of Colorado and Wyoming, in other words, from the Rio Grande to the Pacific Ocean. All this territory was free, when ceded in 1848, by Mexico, but, under the famous 'Compromise of 1850,' slavery was allowed in all the territory except California. So in 1850, the area east of the Rio Grande to the present boundary of Texas on the west and south that had been claimed by Texas, was recognized as forming part of the Territory of New Mexico,—it was slave holding.[7]

April 24th, 1851, the Boundary Commission began active operations to establish the line between the two governments. When they fixed the initial monument at a point on the right bank of the Rio Bravo del Norte at 32° 22', it was made a very solemn occasion. The dignitaries present were, on the part of Mexico, the political chief of Bravos District of the State of Chihuahua, Juan José Sanchez; and in behalf of the United States, Brevet Capt. Abraham Buford, aide-de-camp to James S. Calhoun, who was governor of New Mexico at that time. The operations of this commission were constantly being disturbed; and several changes in authority were made.[8]

When the attempt was made to run the boundary line from the Rio Grande to the Gila River, so many difficulties occurred that on December 30th, 1853, a new treaty was made with Mexico, and the present boundary from the Rio Grande to the Gulf of California was established. Thus there was a new acquisition of land—45,535 square miles—and far south of the Gila. The money that went to Mexico for this additional land was ten million dollars ($10,000,000). The treaty was negotiated by the United States minister to Mexico, James Gadsden, and is known as the Gadsden Purchase; but it is also called the Treaty of Mesilla.

Bancroft tells us that *"The commissioners [Boundary Commission] met in El Paso at the end of 1854, and the initial monument was fixed on January 31, 1855 ... before the end of August [they] completed the survey westward."*[9]

The original boundary had been the Rio Bravo del Norte, but the commission changed the order of things. Don Barbaro Lucero and Adolph Lea, both of Las Cruces, were on this survey, and their description of the method, apparatus, etc., was most interesting. Don Barbaro's statement that flag raising occurred at La Mesilla in July 1854, has been corroborated to me by Messrs. S.G. Bean, Adolph Lea, Horace Stephenson and others.

The flag raising, as described by the above gentlemen, was the confirmation of both treaties, and took place midst a vast crowd in La Mesilla, July 4th, 1854. Troops from Ft. Fillmore, with their commander were there; the Plaza was the scene of action; and Gov. David Meriwether from Santa Fé was present and delivered an address. It was explained very clearly to the people that they were now American citizens; the stars and stripes then were floated from one of the great cotton wood trees, and when a shout went up from the crowds, the ceremony was ended. Of course there was complaint, and some bitterness at the change, but the Mexican population soon adjusted themselves to the new regime and have proved themselves to be good, law-abiding citizens.

Notes:

[1] Bracito, or Brazito, is midway between Chihuahua and Santa Fé, about thirteen days journey from each. *L.L.B.*

[2] George Wilkins Kendall, *Narrative of the Texan Santa Fé Expedition* (London: Wiley and Putnam, 1844. Reprinted by Steck Company, Austin, Texas, 1935), Volume 1: 400.

[3] Brigado-General José Manuel Monterde was born in the Federal District, Mexico in 1789 and died in 1861. In 1842 he led the fighting in northern Chihuahua against the Apaches. As Governor of Chihuahua, he was sent to New Mexico in 1843 as reinforcement against the Texans. While serving as Director del Colegio Militar, he built the fortifications del Castillo de Chapultepec and was later taken prisoner in the battle of September 12-13, 1847. He also signed the *La Venta de La Mesilla*. Francisco R. Almeda, *Diccionario de Historica, Geografia y Biografia Chihuahueuses* (Chihuahua: Talleres Graficas del Gobierno del Estado, 1927), p. 457. *M.E.M.*

[4] 'Rifle-yager:' The U.S. Model 1841 Percussion Rifle was the first regulation muzzle-loading percussion rifle adopted for use by the U.S. Army. *J.T.B.*

[5] McFie included the following footnote as a part of the Hughes text: "It is said that Col. Doniphan and several of his officers and men, were, at this moment, engaged in playing a game of three-trick-loo. At first he observed that the cloud of dust was perhaps produced by a gust of wind and that they had as well play their hands out. In another moment the plumes and banners of the enemy were plainly in view. The colonel quickly sprang to his feet, threw down his cards,

grasped his saber, and observed, 'Boys, I held an invincible hand, but I'll be d-n-d if I don't have to play it out in steel now.' Every man flew to his post." Hughes, *Doniphan's Expedition*, p. 131, footnote 1. *J.T.B.*

[6] John T. Hughes, *Doniphan's Expedition: Containing an Account of the Conquest of Mexico ....* (Cincinnati, U.P. James, 1847) pp. 130-135. The most recent articles on the Battle of Bracito are: Charles M. Haeker, "Brazito Battlefield: Once Lost, Now Found," *New Mexico Historical Review*, 72: 229-238 (July 1997); Neil C. Mangum, "The Battle of Brazito: Reappraising a Lost and Forgotten Episode in the Mexican-American War," *New Mexico Historical Review*, 71: 217-228 (July 1997); and Enrique Tamez Vasquez, "Brazito Remembered One Hundred Fifty Years Ago: Another Loo," *Password*, 43:55-68 (Summer 1998). *J.T.B.*

[7] The question of the Texas-New Mexico boundary is thoroughly explained in Mart J. Stegmaier, *Texas, New Mexico, and the Compromise of 1850* (Kent, Ohio: Kent State University Press, 1996). *J.T.B.*

8 For more on the Boundary Commission and its work see Leon C. Metz, *Border: The U.S: Mexico Line,* (El Paso: Mangan Books, 1989), pp. 11-68. *J.T.B.*

9 Hubert Howe Bancroft, *The Works of Hubert Howe Bancroft, volume XVII: History of Arizona and New Mexico, 1530-1888,* (San Francisco: The History Company, Publishers, 1889), pp. 493-494.

Chapter II

Early New Mexico History

The Mesilla Valley grants are taken up in the order of their dates with one exception; 1st, Santa Teresa; 2nd, Bracito; 3rd, Doña Ana Bend Colony; 4th, Refugio Colony; 5th, La Mesilla Civil Colony Grant; 6th, Santo Tomás de Yturbide Colony; and 7th, Juan Gid, or John C. Heath Grant.[1]

The Refugio Colony and Santa Teresa grants are soon to be resurveyed and slightly reduced; also, the Bracito will be altered somewhat.

In the matter of location Doña Ana is the most northerly of the tracts. Then comes La Mesilla to the southwest; Santo Tomás lies south of La Mesilla; Bracito east of Santo Tomás; Refugio south of Bracito; and last comes Santa Teresa which lies below Refugio and which extends to the borders of both Texas and Mexico.

The Spanish Government issued a number of grants. In the Mesilla Valley are situated two of them, the Santa Teresa and the Bracito. Under the Mexican government come the other four, Doña Ana *Ancon* (or Bend) Colony, La Mesilla Civil Colony, Santo Tomás, and Refugio.[2] Nearly the whole area of the valley was taken up by a bogus grant known as the Juan Gid or John G. Heath Grant. This grant was brought to light a few years ago and created an excitement among grant owners, because it covered every grant except the Doña Ana. It was brought to trial before the Court of Private Land Claims, in Santa Fé, in 1895, and the plaintiffs were defeated.

The colonization laws suffered many alterations, scarcely a year having passed without some change being made; as the head of the country was shifted from shoulder to shoulder, laws were constantly being annulled and new ones enacted. But grants which had been made by Spanish officers were confirmed and held valid by Mexican authorities.[3]

Soldiers were granted the right to claim suertes of land in pueblos by decree of the *Extraordinary Cortes* on January 4th, 1813. The council of each town, the *Ayuntamiento*, was the authority in which power was vested to designate the lands to be given them; also, it was to execute all proceedings relative thereto; that is, to make titles to the lands, and to attend to all proceedings concerning the transaction. All proceedings of the *Ayuntamiento* were ratified by the Provincial Department before they became legal. This was annulled by Royal decree, September 5th, 1814.

Great areas of vacant land remained, and in two years three radical changes in the system of granting were made. The first was on February 24th, 1821, when relations between Spain and Mexico ceased; then under Yturbide was the law of January 4th, 1823, in which the *Ayuntamiento* was all powerful and the approval of the Provincial Deputation was not required. This was soon replaced by the law of August 4th, 1824, which gave powers to governors with subsequent approval of the Territorial Deputation and the Supreme Government.

March 28th, 1828, another set of laws were made referring to foreigners, how they should obtain public lands, and declaring that the law of 1824 "remains in force." April 4th, 1837, the Colonization Laws were repealed and, on the 6th, new ones were enacted. March 11th, 1842, Santa-Anna promulgated a decree relating to foreigners and declared they could not acquire public lands without contract with the general government. Then on May 18th, 1847, Congress went back to the laws of 1823 and 1824. August of the next year, 1848, a decree of the Republic of Mexico and colonization regulations of the Supreme Government of the State of Chihuahua established the office of Commissioner General for removal of Mexican families in the national territory and establishment of civil colonies in that state. The commissioner was Rev. Ramon Ortiz, the curate of El Paso, and a very excellent man as known by early settlers, and who is spoken so highly of both by Cozzens in his book, and by Hon. W.W. Mills, now United States Consul at Chihuahua, in *Forty Years At El Paso.*[4] Father Ortiz officiated at the measurement of the Refugio

Colony Grant and gave titles to all colonists; then, shortly after, retired and Guadalupe Miranda was appointed in his place.

SANTA TERESA: The grant was made by Spanish officials on February 9th, 1768 to Joaquin Mestas and his two married sons. At that time the land lay in Santa Ana County. This tract includes 9,681.29 acres; it lies in the extreme southern corner of the valley; it is crossed by the Southern Pacific Railroad; its boundaries are Mexico on the south, the Rio Grande and Texas on the east, while the Refugio Grant overlaps the northeast corner. The grant was approved December 11th, 1878, but has neither been confirmed nor patented.[5]

BRACITO: The Bracito or Hugh Stephenson Grant is a famous land mark, containing 18,859.48 acres. It lies to the northeast of Santa Teresa, and upon it stand the ruins of old Ft. Fillmore, a seven-company post, built in 1851. The name, derived from the Spanish word *braso* and a diminutive suffix, came from a branch of the Rio Grande extending to the east which stood out prominently in about the center of tract.[6]

The old papers were lost during the war times and data I have received from Hon. Horace Stephenson, of Las Cruces, who is the son of Hugh Stephenson, previously mentioned. Mr. Stephenson says this tract was granted to Juan Antonio Garcia by the Spanish Government in 1818. Hugh Stephenson obtained title to two-thirds interest of said grant from the heirs of Garcia, taking as his portion the upper part. This is the only grant in the valley that has been confirmed. It was approved December 30th, 1856, and confirmed June 21st, 1860.

DOÑA ANA BEND COLONY: This grant is probably the most interesting of any to us because it brought our system of acequias and the first town in the valley. The grantor was Mexico; the grantees the Doña Ana colonists (names of whom are given in another place). The first petition was in September, 1839. The date is July 8th, 1840, and the same was approved on March 31st, 1874. The area of this tract is 35,399.017 acres; it is the most northerly in the valley, 13.25 miles long, and upon it are the old settlements of Doña Ana, Las Cruces, and Tortugas. Antonio Rey, Prefect of El Paso, Guadalupe Miranda and Pablo Melendrez, Sr., surveyed the boundary. All are dead long ago.[7]

This grant brings up the settlement of the town which bears its name and its story is a tale of the utmost interest and novelty. Records show that on July 8th, 1840, a grant was issued by the Mexican Government to a company of Mexican citizens of El Paso, now called Juárez, for the tract of land situated upon the Rio Bravo del Norte, as described above. Though the Government demanded 130 men, only 14 presented themselves on the date set to leave; the start was made, however, and with their provisions, rifles and ammunition upon their shoulders, they arrived at their destination on the second day of February, 1842. The origin of the name of Doña Ana is much disputed, but that of Don Pablo Melendrez [junior] is thought to be the most accurate, as his father, together with José María Costales, was one of the first alcaldes and one of the original colonists, and he, himself, arrived, a small boy, at that place in 1843. His statement is: Doña means lady; Ana, a woman's name; the promise was extracted from some of the party by a woman in El Paso to name the colony after her, and it was done.

The construction of ditches was the first act of the colonists and this work was well done; for, though constructed with wooden spades, hoes, or rather half iron hoes, it took these fourteen an incredibly short time,—for the acequia was eight miles long, the outlet or mouth being just about where Las Cruces stands—was finished by the month of April that same year. Then the men turned their attention to breaking the ground of one piece of land amongst them to raise crops for the winter's consumption. Working in their field was a very dangerous matter, for the Indians were fierce and fairly infested the valley. One half of the men went to the field, heavily armed, one acting as sentinel while the others worked; the other half stayed in town at jacal building or whatever there was to be done. The signal for an attack was a pistol shot, and if the field men fired the shot the town men ran to the rescue; while, if the signal came from the town the workers hastened to the village. No shot under any circumstances was fired except as an Indian warning.

Provisions were brought from El Paso. A most dangerous tedious process it was, for there was not a pack animal in the valley and the settlement could scarcely spare one man, much less the party of six or more who had to go on these excursions.

After a while, the settlers chose another site for their town—a place something a mile or two below the first location, and up above on a high bluff where they were in command of the neighboring country. Here they began at once to build adobe houses. These adobes they had to carry on their back, or in clumsy hand-barrows, a distance of one hundred to one hundred and fifty yards. Water was also transported this way; timber was obtained by chopping trees, and then floating them down on the current, and then dragging or carrying up the hill to their settlement.

It is said to be true of this long-ago town, that so crude was the manner of living that when General Mauricio Ugarte with his troops bound for the north [in 1842 in response to the invasion of Texans] arrived at the settlement, there were but four men to greet the company.[8] These men were Pablo Melendrez, José M. Costales, Geronimo Lujan and José María Bernal. The General inquired for the others and upon learning that they were hidden because they were completely destitute of clothing, he ordered them before him and generously fitted them out with his soldiers' clothing, gave them provisions, and a horse and a mule. Thus came the first two animals to Doña Ana.

All this time there was no other settlement between Socorro and El Paso and there was no priest with them. The next year the families of the settlers came to them.

With the history of Doña Ana a great deal is said about a wonderful rooster which would never utter a sound except when some danger was near. The first fowls came to the town in the possession of Manuel Barregos, and this one rooster proved, on many occasions, such a true prophet that the settlers held it great reverence, listening for his first sound of warning. Instance after instance do the old settlers give of the marvels of the rooster's instinct, and, indeed, it is not remarkable that these simple minded people should become to regard it with such awe; the fowl lived to a good old age and the settlement was grief stricken when the end came.

Don Pablo Melendrez, who had come at the head of the band, held the office of Justice of the Peace—called an *Alcalde*—having been appointed by the Mexican authorities. Don Pablo was in the same office until the Guadalupe Hidalgo treaty and after that, the new authority simply reappointed the same officials to act, except when the town had a military commander. This was done at the time to almost all towns.

Upon his return from the north in 1843 General Mauricio Ugarte stopped in Doña Ana and left a detachment of twenty-five soldiers under Lieut. Trinidad Ollaca, a young six-footer of about twenty-five. After this many settlers moved in, with horses and carts, so that crops were abundant and the town became prosperous.

All this time little affairs with the Indians were constantly annoying the inhabitants; for, no sooner had they declared truce and exchanged liquor for peace, than the Indians would break over, raiding and murdering. Travelers were continually passing through the valley; on one occasion this Lieut. Ollaca returned dressed in a new suit of black cloth and tall black silk hat which he had taken from an Indian whom he had shot. These had been robbed from a man by the name of James Magoffin, who had been attacked about the Bracito country.[9]

About this time the Americans were threatening to come south and the Mexican General Monterde, with a large force arrived at Doña Ana one night. Next day the gallant Ollaca was sent out to scout on the approaching Americans and was met, murdered by the Indians on the Jornada del Muerto, and his body, after being robbed was stood up against a soap weed for crows and scorching sun to mortify.

Thus the American troops found the body, as they approached Doña Ana which had been deserted by the Mexican army. The Americans had for an interpreter, a Frenchman, Frank Fletcher, who had come in 1844; Mr. Fletcher died not very many years ago.

Lieut. [Delos Bennet] Sackett had a command of one hundred cavalry. Between 1842 and 1847 there were about five hundred people in Doña Ana, and the first traveling priest that arrived was Father Quojas in about 1845.

Don Pablo Melendrez [Junior] told me of a bold robbery committed by two Apache and two Isleta Indians. The thieves tore a door in the adobe wall with raw-hide ropes, stole eight Government horses, and though followed the next day, they were not heard of until later, when a wounded Apache came to town and told of a fight that the thieves had among themselves over the division of the horses.

18

This was indeed a rough time; stories there are,—and I have no doubt as to the truth of them,—of wild revenge, cold-blooded greed or so-called justice committed by the Indians, gamblers, even soldiers, or by that rough class, who, eager for adventure, make for the far frontier.

The names of the officers who were in Doña Ana are as follows in order of serving: Lieut. [Delos Bennet]Sackett, Maj. [Enoch] Stein [Steen], Maj. [Oliver L.] Shephard, Capt. [Abraham] Buford, and Lieut. [Lawrence W.] O'Bannon.

The names of the fourteen colonists are: Pablo Melendrez, Sr., José M. Costales, Juan José Benavidas, Francisco Rodrigues, Jesus Olivarez, José María Bernal, José María Perea, Francisco Lucero, Geronimo Lujan, Saturnino Abillar, José Ines Garcia, Gabriel Babalos, Ramon de la Serna, and one other.

REFUGIO COLONY GRANT: No. 90 is the Refugio Colony Grant made by Mexico in the year 1851 or 1852, to Refugio colonists led by José María Garcia. It was approved on May 18th, 1874, contains 26,130.19 acres, and lies with one corner overlapping the Santa Teresa on the south, the present bed of the Rio Grande runs almost through the middle, the old bed its eastern boundary. On the north, the distance of four miles and sixty chains to the Bracito is covered by United States patents. This tract is twelve miles long, and on it are the towns of Chamberino, La Union, Bailey's Ranch, and the old settlement known as Los Amoles, with just across the boundary (old river bed) Anthony and the ranch of Jesus Ochoa.[10]

In 1852, two allotments were made: one was to José de la Luz Jaquez, one square league; the other, to José María Garcia. Ramon Ortiz, curate of Paso del Norte, and Commissioner of the Mexican Government to found and establish colonies in the State of Chihuahua from New Mexico, was the one under whom the colonists took possession of the land; he was shortly after succeeded by Guadalupe Miranda.

SANTO TOMÁS de YTERBIDE GRANT: This grant of only 9,598.60 acres lies directly south of the La Mesilla Civil Grant. It was formally assigned to Guadalupe Miranda, August 3rd, 1853, but as it has never been even approved, and, as there was only one old faded blue print of the tract in the possession of the Court of Private Land Claims, I could not get much data on it. However, anyone traveling along the bottoms about two miles south of La Mesilla will run across the ruins of Santo Tomás village. The Rio Grande runs practically through the middle. This grant was made by the Mexican Government. The lands embraced there were set apart to the people composing the colony of Santo Tomás de Yterbide by Guadalupe Miranda, General Commissioner of the Mexican Government for removal of families and regulation of colonies.[11]

LA MESILLA CIVIL COLONY: This valuable tract was a Mexican grant made in 1853, August 4th, to the La Mesilla colonists. It extends up the valley to a place above the little old town of Picacho to Apache Ford *Ancon* (meaning bend). It was approved February 12th, 1874, slightly before the Refugio Grant which was approved at the same term of Congress, and contains 21,628.52 acres of land. La Mesilla, the interesting old town on the river, has been one of the most important places of the frontier, and its sandy ruins are eloquent of the past. Mr. Adolph Lea describes that portion of the valley as a thick jungle of trees and shrubs where the men used to hunt all sorts of big game.[12]

LA MESILLA

La Mesilla, until the final change of the river in 1865, was upon the west side of the river, and it was founded shortly after the treaty of Guadalupe Hidalgo in 1848, when Mexico threw her gates open to receive back her people who had gone up into United States territory and settled. The treaty provided that those who remained on United States ground for a year after the treaty would become citizens of the Union,—or as Hon. [Samuel W.] Sherfey cleverly expressed it: "It required some activity to get out of being a citizen at that time,"—and those who returned to Mexico within the same time received grants of land for a homestead. Thus the whole of Northern Mexico was thrown open, and those returning settlers arriving at the nearest point—the Rio Grande being the line—settled in colonies all down the river.

Other towns down the river resulting from the same cause are Santo Tomás, San Miguel, Chamberino, Nombre de Dios, La Union and, quite probably, La Mesa.

La Mesilla immediately became a booming town, which in 1851 was improved greatly in commerce and importance by the building of Ft. Fillmore.

On August 4th, 1853, Guadalupe Miranda arrived at La Mesilla, measured off the limits of the La Mesilla Civil Colony Grant, and issued titles to all land owners.

La Mesilla was governed by *alcaldes*, as was Doña Ana. It came into the Union by the Gadsden Purchase; the flag was raised in 1854, as described elsewhere, and all officers who were loyal to the Americans were left in their former positions.

In speaking of this settlement as it looked in 1853 when he, a young boy, was on his way east to college, Hon. Horace Stephenson says:

I do not think there were twelve houses in La Mesilla then. It was a very large heavily populated town, but the houses were all jacals; even the church was only a jacal, and was situated then on the east side of the Plaza, opposite from where it is now.

Twice, people have migrated from La Mesilla in bodies. The reason of the first departure 1862 was that before the river became so fickle and finally changed its bed, and for fully three years after this disturbance, the ditches could not be gotten in order, many farmers were starved out and, becoming discouraged, removed and settled to the north, the towns of Colorado and Santa Barbara; and, to the east, Tularosa and La Luz.

A second departure occurred as the result of the great political riot in 1873, when John Lemon, the Republican leader, was brutally murdered on the Plaza near the southwest corner of the church. This company was led by Ignacio Orantio, and the dissatisfied people made their home in Mexico, calling the place La Acención.

This is a very famous old town. Three times she has been the scene of changes in national government, and many dark deeds have been perpetrated in and around its adobe corrals and fields.

DR. JOHN G. HEATH, or JUAN GID GRANT: This most interesting case, was decided by the U.S. Court of Private Land Claims at the December term, 1884, at Santa Fe, N.M. The tract was a huge one, embracing one hundred and thirty thousand acres, and would have swallowed nearly the whole of this valley. Taking the head of the Bracito *acequia* as the central point of a square five leagues each way with one corner at La Cueva—that pile of crags at the feet of the Organ Mountains—and another away south upon a hill to the right of the Trujillo Salt Lakes, though somewhat in advance of them, and opposite the last ridge of the El Paso mountain called *Puerto de Los Alamitos* one gets an idea of the wealth and interest this case aroused.[13]

The plaintiffs, descendants of the grantee in this, Dr. John G. Heath or Juan Gid, as the Spanish has it—and all the business was done under this Spanish signature—were J.B. and Kate B. Cessna, and John B. and May Keedle. These plaintiffs allege that Dr. John G. Heath, was an Anglo-American from the State of Missouri, having become a Mexican citizen, a Roman Catholic, and taken up his residence in El Paso, State of Chihuahua, Mexico, made application for a tract of land, in proper legal form to the *Ayuntamiento* of El Paso del Norte, on April 3rd, 1823. After the surveying and various requirements were satisfied, and immediately upon the grant of the said tract, Dr. John G. Heath went to the United States to procure his stores, merchandise, medicines, implements of husbandry, and thirty Roman Catholic families, according to the contract. This he did at the expense of $8,000.00, and taking them to Mexico as provided, and on arriving on said premises found that the revolutionary government that succeeded the authorities that had made him the grant forbade him remaining on the premises, for the grant was issued under the laws of 1823, and shortly afterward when the government went to pieces and Yterbide was shot and killed, the laws were repealed. All then returned to the United States, so plead the plaintiffs, but their cause was decided against them by the Court. However, many points of international interest were brought out in the case and it is so absorbing that one could write a book upon it alone.

MILITARY AND TERRITORIAL RULE

In 1846, when Kearny demanded the oath of allegiance from the officials at Santa Fé, and Governor [Donaciano] Vigil delivered a brief address, giving it in the name of his people, was the time when military government of the United States was established in New Mexico. It was the policy of the United States Government to establish temporary civil government and where officers were friendly to our government to leave them in charge; so Vigil's rule continued. Kearny's proclamation ignored the fact that the eastern part—the eastern side of the Rio Grande—belonged to Texas.

The treaty of Guadalupe Hidalgo gave the people a choice of citizenship between two governments, and the military regime was at an end, so Governor Vigil ruled on until October 1848.

The government, run by the governor, legislature and military officers, was an uncertain element; our valley was too thinly populated to have any representation, so things went calmly along between alcaldes and the military stationed here. The Gadsden Purchase moved the boundary line southward to include all of modern Arizona south of the Gila.

Under the treaty of 1848 the commissioners had agreed on latitude 32° 22' as the southern boundary, which gave a part of this valley to Mexico; but the United States surveyor would not accept this, and he had another survey made at 31° 54', for the New Mexicans claimed the Mesilla Valley which lay between the two lines as part of their territory. Mexico, who was badly in need of money, made the sale, and this small and comparatively unimportant part of the boundary dispute was amicably settled, though for a time war seemed inevitable, and thus no portion of this valley was either in Mexico or in Texas.

Doña Ana County was organized on January 6th, 1852.

In 1853 Doña Ana County had her first sheriff, a man residing in Las Cruces today, S.G. Bean. His term of office was eight years and to use Mr. Bean's own description of the district over which he was supposed to keep law and order:

My jurisdiction was not as large as the Czar of Russia's, including Siberia, but it extended from Texas 300 miles to the east and to California 700 miles to the west, or in other words, it was 1000 miles long by 300 wide.

The list of sheriffs for Doña Ana County up till the present one has been supplied me by Hon. S.G. Bean, the first sheriff.

S.G. Bean	eight years
Marcial Padilla	two years
Fabian Gonzalez	two years
Apolina Barela	two years
Mariano Barela	four years
Eugene Van Patten	two years
James Ascarate	two years
G[uadalupe] Ascarate	two years
James Southwick	two years
Martin Lohman	two years
Patrick Garrett	four years
José Lucero	two years

Very little was the law and order maintained during this time. I could only learn indirectly of an irregular administration of justice in La Mesilla or Tucson.

The earliest records of the county in the Recorder's Office in Las Cruces were begun in 1853; J.S. Tucker was county clerk, September 18th and the first deed, a plat of Las Cruces. The gentleman in charge at present, Mr. Isidor Armijo, informed me that the records prior to 1853 were supposed to have been kept by Curé Ramon Ortiz, the Mexican Commissioner in Juárez.

In 1854 we find Richard Campbell the Probate Judge. At Las Cruces was established the first county seat, but as no court house was built, court was held in some building on Main Street.

Early in the fifties come the first district court records, when the first session of court was an hour or so long, and a brass band and general jollification occupied the rest of the day. *El Gringo, or New Mexico and Her People* written by W.W.H. Davis in July 1856, contains an account of his first term of court in Doña Ana County. Mr.

Davis was U.S. attorney under Judge [Kirby] Benedict; the county seat was situated at Las Cruces. Court convened in March one Monday morning and lasted until Friday afternoon. The court officials stayed at a public house owned by Mr. T[homas] J. Bull. Little attention was ever paid to the court, it seems, and even as late as 1855, when Judge [Joseph G.] Knapp was on the bench.[14] *"Military authority was almost supreme,"* wrote Senator S[tephen] B. Elkins, among other things, in response to my questions upon the early government of the valley. The county seat was then in La Mesilla.[15]

While the county seat was at La Mesilla, the little old stone jail, recently torn down, had held many prisoners behind its bars; probably the most noted was Billy the Kid, or William Bonney as his true name was.[16] On the walls inside this old jail were some curious stone-cut characters and a tracery of a horse; these were the handiwork of this man. He was captured and lodged there early in 1881, and was taken from La Mesilla by Deputy United States Marshall Robert Olinger, Deputy Sheriff David Woods and others, and turned over, April 21st, to Sheriff P[atrick] F. Garrett who was then in office. Billy was turned over at Ft. Stanton, nine miles west of Lincoln because Lincoln County then had no jail. Chief Deputy J.T. Bell and Robert Olinger took charge of the prisoner.

About 6:30 on the afternoon of the 28th of April, one week after his arrival, Billy effected his escape after killing both Bell and Olinger. As we know, Billy the Kid met his death at the hands of Sheriff Garrett.[17]

The occasion of the change of the county seat to La Mesilla from Las Cruces was that the former had a greater number of voters than the latter, so the office was moved. Bitterness was very strong over this change. The office remained there until the early 80's when the railroad was put through Las Cruces—and would have gone through La Mesilla had it not been for the astonishing opposition of the most prominent man, Hon. Thomas Bull. People would not submit to attending court off the railroad, so an act of the legislature was passed to move it to Las Cruces. There was feeling over this act and people went so far as to take a vote, but the records were moved over directly.

Horace Stephenson was then in office, and as there was no court house and the authorities had not waited to build one, the office was set up in the old portion of the building now occupied by the public school. Court was then held in the large hall of the old Amador Hotel, which is standing yet, in the south end of town. In 1884 the court house was built and, when new, was a handsome and costly building.

By act of Congress, August 4th, 1854, this Gadsden Purchase territory was added to New Mexico. Arizona had no settlement. There existed hardly the semblance of county jurisdiction, as by act of the legislature, January 18th, 1855, it was attached to Doña Ana County. We were then in Doña Ana County, Arizona.

In 1860, from the 2nd to the 5th of April, there was held at Tucson a constitutional convention composed of 31 delegates which proceeded to "ordain and establish" a provisional constitution to remain in force "until congress shall reorganize a territorial government and no longer." This new territory included all of New Mexico south of latitude 33° 40' and was divided by north and south lines into four counties. A governor was elected in the person of Dr. L. S. Owings of Mesilla; three judicial districts were created, the judges to be appointed by the government.[18]

This resulted in nothing. The following, dated La Mesilla, Ariz., June 14th, 1861, is so peculiar a document and so characteristic of the times, that I print it entire.

Dr. Lorenzo Labadi,
> *Las Cruces, N.Mex.*
> *The sixth resolution of a Convention held in the city of Mesilla, Ariz., the 16th day of March, 1861, is as follows:*
> *Resolved that we will not recognize the present Black Republican administration, and that we will resist any officers appointed to this Territory by said administration with whatever means in our power.*
> *A true copy.*
>> *Jas. A. Lucas,*
>> *Pres. of the Convention*
Attested, Ch. S.A. Happin, Secretary[19]

The man to whom this notification was addressed was the U.S. Indian Agent from near Tucson; the paper was handed him while in Las Cruces by a party of citizens of La Mesilla,—a printer by the name of Kelly, of whom we will hear later, and three other men. They threatened to tar and feather him if he attempted to exercise the duties of his office. Mr. Labadi appealed to Brevet Maj. G.R. Paul of the U.S.A., who was then commanding Ft. Fillmore, and was promised military protection should any attempt be made against his person.

Next we find ourselves a confederate territory under Colonel Baylor, who issued the following proclamation:

Proclamation

To the People of the Territory of Arizona:

The social and political condition of Arizona being little short of general anarchy, and the people being literally destitute of law, order and protection, the said Territory, from the date hereof, is hereby declared temporarily organized as a military government until such time as Congress may otherwise provide.

I, John R. Baylor, lieutenant-colonel, commanding the Confederate Army in the Territory of Arizona, hereby take possession of the said Territory in the name and behalf of the Confederate States of America.

For all the purposes herein specified, and until otherwise decreed or provided, the Territory of Arizona shall comprise all that portion of New Mexico lying south of the thirty-fourth parallel of north latitude.

All offices, both civil and military, heretofore existing in this Territory, either under the laws of the late United States or the Territory of New Mexico, are hereby declared vacant, and from the date hereof shall forever cease to exist.

That the people of this Territory may enjoy the full benefits of law, order, and protection, and, as far as possible, the blessings and advantages of a free government, it is hereby decreed that the laws and enactments existing in this Territory prior to the date of this proclamation, and consistent with the Constitution and laws of the Confederate States of America and the provisions of this decree, shall

*continue in full force and effect without interruption, until such time
as the Confederate Congress may otherwise provide.*

*The said Territory of Arizona from the date hereof is hereby tem-
porarily organized under a military government until such time as
Congress may otherwise provide. The said government shall be
divided into two separate and distinct departments, to wit: The
executive and judicial. The executive authority of this Territory shall
be vested in the commandant of the Confederate Army of Arizona.
The judicial power of this Territory shall be vested in a supreme
court, two district courts, two probate courts, and a justice of the
peace, together with such municipal and other inferior courts as the
wants of the people may from time to time require. The two district
judges shall constitute the supreme court, each of whom shall deter-
mine all appeals, exceptions, and writs of error removed from the
district court wherein the other presides. One of said judges shall be
designated as the chief justice of the supreme court. There shall be
but one session each year, which shall be holden at the seat of government. The district judges shall hold two terms of court every year
in their respective judicial districts. They may like wise hold special
terms whenever in their opinion the ends of public justice require it.*

*The judicial districts of the Territory shall be divided as follows:
The first judicial district shall comprise all the portion of Arizona
lying east of the Apache Pass, the district and probate courts whereof
shall be holden at La Mesilla. The second judicial district shall comprise the remainder of the Territory. The district and probate courts
shall be holden at Tucson. The governor shall likewise appoint one
probate judge and sheriff and the necessary justices of the peace in
and for each judicial district ... Each district judge shall appoint his
own clerk, who shall be ex officio clerk of the probate court within
such district. The district and probate courts of the two districts shall
be holden at such times as heretofore provided by the legislature of
New Mexico for the counties of Doña Ana and Arizona.*

*All suits and other business now pending in any of the late courts
of New Mexico within this Territory shall be immediately transferred
to the corresponding courts of the Territory, as herein established.
The style for all process shall be the Territory of Arizona and all
prosecutions shall be carried on in the name of the Territory of Arizona.*

There shall likewise be appointed by the governor an attorney-general, secretary of the Territory, treasurer, and marshal, whose duty and compensation shall be the same as heretofore under the laws of New Mexico.

The city of Mesilla is hereby designated as the seat of government of this Territory.

All Territorial officers shall hold their respective terms of office until otherwise provided by Congress, unless sooner removed by the power appointing them.

The salaries, fees, and compensation of all Territorial officers shall remain the same as heretofore in the Territory of New Mexico.

The treasurer, marshal, sheriffs, and constables, before acting as such, shall execute to the Territory a bond, with good and sufficient securities, conditioned for the faithful discharge of their official duties, in the same manner as heretofore provided under the laws of New Mexico.

All Territorial officers, before entering upon their official duties shall take an oath or affirmation to support the Constitution and laws of the Confederate States and of this Territory and faithfully to discharge all duties incumbent upon them.

The bill of rights of the Territory of New Mexico, so far as consistent with the Constitution and laws of the Confederate States and the provisions of this decree, are hereby declared to full force and effect in the Territory of Arizona.

Given under my hand at Mesilla this 1st day of August, 1861.
John R. Baylor,
Gov. and Lieut. Col. Comdg. Mounted Rifles, C.S. Army[20]

Appointments

In accordance with the provisions of a proclamation, dated August 1, 1861, organizing temporarily the Territory of Arizona, I, John R. Baylor, governor of said Territory, do hereby publish and declare the following appointments. All appointees are requested to qualify and enter upon their official duties without delay:

Secretary of the Territory, James A. Lucas; attorney general, M.H. McWillie; treasurer, E. Augorstein; marshal, George M. Frazier;

probate judge first judicial district, Frank Higgins; justice of the peace Doña Ana County, L.W. Greek; justice of the peace Mesilla, fourth precinct, M.A. Verimendi; justice of the peace Mesilla, fifth precinct, Henry L. Dexter; justice of the peace La Mesa, Theodor J. Miller; justice of the peace, Pinos Altos, M.M. Steinthal; justice of the peace, San Tomas, C. Lanches

Given under my hand at Mesilla
this 2nd day of August, A.D. 1861.
John R. Baylor,
Gov. and Lieut. Col. Comdg. Mounted Rifles, C.S. Army[21]

A few months later the following proclamation was issued.

<u>Proclamation of Brig. Gen. H. H. Sibley,</u>
<u>Army of the Confederate States,</u>
<u>to the people of New Mexico</u>

An army under my command enters New Mexico, to take posses-sion of it in the name and for the benefit of the Confederate States. By geographical position, and by similarity of institutions, by com-mercial interests, and by future destinies New Mexico pertains to the Confederacy.

Upon the peaceful people of New Mexico the Confederate States wage no war. To them we come as friends to re-establish a govern-mental connection agreeable and advantageous both to them and to us; to liberate them from the yoke of a military despotism erected by usurpers upon the ruins of the former free institutions of the United States; to relieve them from the iniquitous taxes and exactions imposed upon them by that usurpation; to insure and to revere their religion, and to restore their civil and political liberties.

The existing war is one most wickedly waged by the United States upon the Confederate States for the subjugation and oppression of the latter by force of arms. It has already failed. Victory has crowned the arms of the Confederate States wherever an encounter worthy of being called a battle has been joined. Witness the battles of Bull Run, of Manassas, of Springfield, of Lexington, of Leesburg, of

Columbus, and the capture in the Mesilla Valley of the whole force of the enemy by scarcely half their number.

The army under my command is ample to seize and to maintain possession of New Mexico against any force which the enemy now has or is able to place within its limits. It is my purpose to accomplish this object without injury to the peaceful people of the country. Follow, then, quietly your peaceful avocations, and from my forces you have nothing to fear. Your persons, your families, and your property shall be secure and safe. Such forage and supplies as my army shall require will be purchased in open market and paid for at fair prices. If destroyed or removed to prevent me from availing myself of them, those who so co-operate with our enemies will be treated accordingly, and must prepare to share their fate.

It is well known to me that many among you have already been forced by intimidation or inveigled by fraud into the ranks of our foes. The day will soon arrive when you can safely abjure their service. When it comes, throw down your arms and disperse to your homes, and you are safe. But persist in the service, and you are lost.

When the authority of the Confederate States shall be established in New Mexico, a government of your best men, to be conducted upon principles with which you are familiar and to which you are attached, will be inaugurated. Your religious, civil, and political rights and liberties will be re-established and maintained sacred and intact. In the meantime, by virtue of the powers vested in me by the President and Government of the Confederate States I abrogate and abolish the law of the United States levying taxes upon the people of New Mexico.

To all my old comrades in arms, still in the ranks of the usurpers of their Government and liberties, I appeal in the name of the former friendship: drop at once the arms which degrade you into the tools of tyrants, renounce their service, and array yourselves under the colors of justice and freedom! I am empowered to receive you into the service of the Confederate States; the officers upon their commissions, the men upon their enlistments. By every principle of law and morality you are exonerated from service in the ranks of our enemies. You never engaged in the service of one portion of the old Union to fight against another portion, who, so from being your enemies, have ever been your best friends. In the sight of God and man, you are justified in renouncing a service iniquitous in itself and in which you never engaged.

Done at headquarters of the Army of New Mexico by me this 20th day of December, A. D., 1861.

H. H. Sibley,
Brigadier General, Army C.S.[22]

In February, 1863, Arizona was made a separate territory, its present boundaries fixed, officials appointed, and on December 27th, the officers headed by Gov. John N. Goodwin, of Maine, entered the territory and the flag was raised.

After the close of the Rebellion, with the return of the Unionists came changes in population and officers, and La Mesilla was no longer a capital.

The Mesilla Valley was never a port of entry. The nearest customs district is that of El Paso del Norte, which was created by Congress, August 2nd, 1854, and was, in part, in these words:

That county of El Paso, in the State of Texas, and the Territory of New Mexico be and they hereby are created a collection district which shall be called the district of Paso del Norte and Frontera, within said county of El Paso, is hereby made a port of entry and delivery for said district.[23]

El Paso was the residence of the first collector, Caleb Sherman, and he was followed in 1858 by Col. S[amuel] J. Jones who, by some special act was allowed the privilege of living in Las Cruces.

Early in 1863, W.W. Mills became the collector and he was instrumental in having passed an act of Congress which caused the Collector's office to be removed to El Paso.[24]

Frontera, seven miles above El Paso, was never the residence of a collector for it was merely a sheep ranch, with only one house.

Since the rebellion, this valley has been very turbulent politically. The county seat trouble—already described—ended about 1881, and the valley government has been comparatively peaceful since.

STAGES

1857 was the establishing of the Great Overland Mail line from Southwest Missouri to San Francisco, Cal. It was a great enterprise, established in co-operation with the Government and promoted and managed by an eastern man by the name [John] Butterfield; this level-headed man did his work well, and in honor of his good work the stage system was called the 'Butterfield Route.'[25]

At that time, it will be remembered, the river ran east of La Mesilla about four hundred yards and west of Fort Fillmore about the same distance.

As the old Concord coach, with its mail and passengers swung into the Mesilla Valley, the road came from Texas up through the bottoms on the east side of the Rio Grande to Fort Fillmore; here mail was exchanged, and the road led on up the river for about three miles —or about midway between Fort Fillmore and Mesilla Park—then after fording, met and followed the wagon road into La Mesilla. At this place was located the Home Station and Headquarters of the Route. The exact building where the station was, was on the east of the main street, nearly opposite the store of Thomas Bull; it is still standing.[26]

After a stoppage to exchange mail, etc. the route continued its way up the valley to the town of Picacho, and from there made an angle westward to 'Rough and Ready' station, which lay twenty miles from the Rio Grande. From this point the road ran on an almost straight line to San Francisco.

The fare from start to finish was $150.00, meals being provided by the company at stations, and forty pounds of baggage was allowed. At each station a guard of six or seven men (at $75.00 and board per month) was kept to look out for relays of horses; the station keeper receiving a salary of $125.00.

This was of immediate benefit to the valley, not only in transporting outsiders and mail, but because the Company purchased all its provisions from the villagers, thus setting into circulation plenty of money. This was a tri-weekly line.

Money in those days was more than plentiful. Congress sent a supervisor from Washington with an appropriation of $100,000.00

for a wagon road. This man made his headquarters at La Mesilla, also paid the men there. Many thrilling times were the lot of the brave men who undertook to act as drivers and conductors on those old Concord coaches, and one of the greatest events in the annals of the Valley was the time when the test coaches arrived at the station.

It seems that after the route was all stocked, and in running gear a wager was made between two persons as to the time of passage; the money staked was large, and on the same day and hour from St. Louis and San Francisco coaches started. The following is a description as given by Hon. Samuel G. Bean, who at the time was Post Master, a storekeeper and hotel man.

We were told we might look for the stages from both ways on the tenth day from the time they started, but this we could hardly believe. Men were sent out on horse back to meet the coach from San Francisco, but came back from the first trip unsuccessful. They went out again. Finally a rider who seemed to have the fleetest horse came dashing into the Plaza, throwing his hat in wild glee—his horse dripping with sweat, yelling, 'She is coming only four miles off, and on a dead tilt.' By this time the Plaza was filled with people and they did not have long to wait until the coach came tearing in; people were wild with joy; as the driver drove into the Plaza he waved his hat with a yell. By this time the square was jammed with people, and the yells from such a multitude were loud and deafening; they shouldered the driver and carried him around and attempted to shoulder the horses. Cries of 'Old Fellow, are you dry? Let's go and take a drink,' were in many mouths.

So far no news had come from St. Louis, but in a few minutes the cry was that it had reached El Paso, forty miles below.

Referring to Indian yells, none of us had ever seen a college or heard of college yells, but we had learned the Indians yells to perfection.

None of us had ever seen a railroad; one of the boys said "Say this is the only railroad we ever will see in this backwoods country."

That coach driver and even horses were objects of interest to the people. Some of them cut a lock of hair from the driver's head and almost wanted to cut the coach for relics. But the coach did not linger long, for with fresh mules and driver it rode on to meet the coach from St. Louis. That long and difficult trip of 1200 miles which emigrants had tugged and worried to make in 60 days, and had done the same on horseback in 40 days, by a Concord had been accomplished in 10 days.

The driver and conductor were the only crew aboard, and, how fearful it seemed, to plunge into a wilderness of country infested by thousands of demons. Think of those two men struggling through nights of inky darkness and not an accident on all that long trip.

The worst tribe of Indians on the route was led by Chief Cochise; they lived in the vicinity of the largest station on the line. The company soon found it wise to conciliate the chief, so orders were given each station keeper to hand over whatever was asked for. Thus a treaty with Cochise and his numerous family was made which lasted for years—until the black rumblings of the Civil War made the Indians restless and eager for plunder.

The outbreak occurred in 1861 at Apache Pass Station in Arizona which is Fort Bowie now. The first act of the Indians was to watch and capture two men from the Station, to revenge a young brave who had lost his life at the station a short time before. The troops had, at that time, four Indian murderers, and within sight of each other, the two companies being on opposite hills, a most hideous scene was enacted, for six lives left six bodies, the two Americans' by burning at the hands of the Indians, and four Indians by hanging at the hands of the soldiers. This fearful tragedy was related to me by Hon. S.G. Bean, of Las Cruces.

Thousands of Indians had gathered to witness this, and, at the provocation of five lives lost, they commenced a series of the most fearful ravages imaginable. The drivers were shot off their boxes, horses cut loose and captured, coaches stranded in mid-desert until the company was forced to move its line north, and a great sorrow prevailed. This went on until about 1876. The Southern Pacific Railroad now runs upon the old stage line.

It was during the second administration of President U.S. Grant, and through his deep study and influence, that the solution of the Indian problem came about. A treaty was consummated and reservations laid out and supplied.

Beside the Overland or Butterfield Route, a continuation of the Old Santa Fé Trail, came into the valley from the north across the Jornada del Muerto, and ran down into Texas. It ran a little this side [east] of Fort Selden, and kept below the sand bluffs in the bottom on this [east] side of the river, the crossing was made near White's Ranch in the extreme south.

From the east another road came into the valley from the El Paso road which ran on the opposite side of the Organ Mountains. It came through that small break in the mountain, known as 'Alamito Pass,' about on an even line with the lower edge of Bracito Grant. From the west and after the Rebellion, the old Silver City and Pinos Altos route was started; it has also been called 'La Linea Visoria.' The Rio Bravo, or Rio Grande, as it is better known, was very high then, and except in dry seasons, everything had to be ferried over, a well-known ferrying station was near Fort Selden, and the best fording, when practicable, near Ft. Fillmore. Thus, at one time and another roads from four points of the compass have entered Mesilla Valley.

Notes:

[1] The sources from which I obtained my data upon the subjects below treated of are: *New Mexico Lands Grants*, 49-104; Vol 2; U.S. Surveyor General's Office, Santa Fé, N.M.; U.S. Court of Private Land Claims (Clerk's Office); *The Legislative Blue-Book of the Territory of New Mexico*, compiled by Hon. W.G. Rich, Secretary of the Territory (Santa Fé: Charles W. Greene, Public Printer, 1882. (reprinted by the University of New Mexico Press, Albuquerque, 1968); Messrs. Horace Stephenson and Pablo Melendrez. *M.E.M.*

2 The José Manuel Sánchez Baca Grant, which McFie does not mention, was a Mexican grant made June 5, 1853. The claim was filed March 24, 1856, and approved May 20, 1882. It was confirmed on September 11, 1900. In the U.S. Surveyor General's Records it is Report #129, File 34. It is Docket #138 in the Court of Private Land Claims records. These records can be found in *The Spanish Archives of New Mexico [microfilm]. Series 1, Surveyor General Records and the Records of the Court of Private Land Claims* (Santa Fé: New Mexico State Records Center and Archives, 1982-1987), hereafter referred to as *Surveyor General Records. J.T.B.*

[3] For more information on land grants, see John R. Van Ness and Christine Van Ness, *Spanish and Mexican Land Grants in New Mexico and Colorado* (Manhattan, Kansas: Sunflower Press, 1980); and J.J. Bowden, *Spanish and Mexican*

Land Grants in the Chihuahuan Acquisition (El Paso: Texas Western Press, 1971). *J.T.B.*

4 Samuel Woodward Cozzens, *The Marvelous Country, or, Three Years in Arizona and New Mexico* ... (Boston: Lee and Shepard, 1846), pp. 47-48; W.W. Mills, *Forty Years at El Paso, 1858-1898* (El Paso, n.p., 1901), p. 20.

5 The Santa Teresa grant was confirmed June 1, 1902. *Surveyor General Records*, Report #111, File #115, Court of Private Land Claims Docket #168.

6 *Surveyor General Records*, Report #6, file #32.

7 The Doña Ana Bend Colony Grant was confirmed April 1, 1897, *Surveyor General Records*, Report #85, File #161, Court of Private Land Claims Docket #24.

8 Col. Mauricio Ugarte was a Mexican army officer, an Indian fighter and politician. From 1835 to 1842 he served as *Jefe Politico* of Paso del Norte. In 1844 he was serving as Inspector de Colonias Militarias and he became acting governor of Chihuahua in the spring of 1848. When the Mexican American War broke out, Ugarte rushed north to help Governor Manuel Armijo but got no further than Doña Ana, returning south before the Battle of Bracito. Almeda, *Diccionario de Historica*, p. 723. *M.E.M.*

9 See Susan Shelby Magoffin, *Down the Santa Fe Trail and in Mexico* (New Haven: Yale University Press, 1926), pp. 151, 200-201. *J.T.B.*

10 The Refugio Colony Grant was confirmed on July 13, 1903. *Surveyor General Records*, Report #90, File #168, Court of Private Land Claims Docket #150.

11 The Santo Tomás de Yterbide Grant was confirmed September 1, 1900. *Surveyor General Records*, Report #139, File #201.

12 The La Mesilla Civil Colony Grant was confirmed September 1, 1900. *Surveyor General Records*, Report #86, File #162, Court of Private Land Claims Docket #151.

13 Case No. 59. For more on Dr. John Heath and the Bracito Grant see Albert Quillen, "El Paso's Lost Colony," *Password*, 43: 69-84 (Summer 1998). *J.T.B.*

14 W.W.H. Davis, *El Gringo or New Mexico and Her People* (n.p., 1857, Reprinted by Rio Grande Press, Chicago, 1962), pp. 217-219.

15 The county seat was originally in Las Cruces. It was moved to Mesilla after the Civil War. Then in 1882 it was moved back to Las Cruces. *J.T.B.*

16 This building stood in Mesilla on the east side of the Plaza on the northeast

corner with Calle de Parian. Currently (1998) it is the Billy The Kid Store. Information on the 1998 locations of historic sites has been learned from Anne E. Kapp, Guylyn M. Nusom, editors, *The Las Cruces Historical Buildings Survey* (Las Cruces: Doña Ana County Historical Society and the City of Las Cruces, 1982), and from various historic maps in the Special Collections, New Mexico State University. *J.T.B.*

[17] The best recent account of Billy the Kid is Robert M. Utley, *Billy the Kid: A Short and Violent Life* (Lincoln: University of Nebraska Press, 1989. *J.T.B.*

[18] Bancroft, *History of Arizona and New Mexico*, pp. 506-507. *J.T.B.*

[19] *The War of the Rebellion: A Compilation of the Official Records of the Union and Confederate Armies* (Washington: Government Printing Office, 1882), Series 1, Volume IV: 39.

[20] *The War of the Rebellion*, IV: 20-21.

[21] *The War of the Rebellion*, IV: 22.

[22] *The War of the Rebellion*, IV: 89-90.

[23] U.S. Statutes: "An Act creating a Collection District in Texas and New Mexico," August 2, 1854.

[24] See Mills, *Forty Years at El Paso*, p. 80; U.S. Statutes: "An Act to facilitate the Collection of Revenue in El Paso County, Texas, and in the Territory of New Mexico," March 3, 1863. *J.T.B.*

[25] See Roscoe P. Conklin and Margaret B. Conklin, *The Butterfield Overland Mail* (Glendale: Arthur H. Clark Co., 1947). *J.T.B.*

[26] The first Butterfield stage stop, 1858-1861, was in the building on the south side of the Plaza, now (1998) occupied by the El Patio Bar and Restaurant and the Nambé shop. It was then moved across Calle de Guadalupe to the southeast corner of the Plaza and Calle de Parian. The building is now occupied by La Posta Restaurant. *J.T.B.*

Chapter III

Development of the Mesilla Valley

This little valley, about forty miles long, the garden spot of southern Doña Ana County, lies on both sides of the river as it flows due south.

The Principal Meridian of New Mexico passes through the Mesilla Valley about five or six miles west of Las Cruces, and probably through this side of Picacho; the meridian is 106° 53' 40" west of Greenwich. The latitude of the college is 32° 18' north.

The Mesilla Valley is bounded on the north by a place where the river has cut through the Doña Ana and Ft. Selden Mountains, leaving steep bluffs on either side, with barely room enough for the railroad track to skirt the hills, this place is called Los Altos, or another name is San Diego, and lies north of the now deserted old town of Leasburg, about six or seven miles north of Fort Selden. The western limit is Picacho Mountain at the northern end, and the long level hills, of Lomas and Lava Mesa, or 'Mal Pais,' ending in the high bluffs on the borders of Mexico and Texas. At the foot of these hills, and marking our southern limit, is an old forsaken place known as White's Ranch. White's Ranch with Garcia's and Fletcher's were famous in the olden times.[1] The beautiful Organ Mountains and the southern continuation of the plains called the Jornada del Muerto form the eastern boundary. The valley under its present system of irrigation, taking from a point in the Selden Mountains to [the] New Mexico and Texas line, contains an area of 70,000 irrigable acres. This makes the valley about forty miles long, and on an average of three miles wide. If all the mesa up to the Organs on the East and Jornada on the northwest, were taken the acreage would be very much larger,—it would give an average width of almost ten miles.

The most prominent town in the valley is Las Cruces.

In 1848, the present site of Las Cruces was surveyed off by an Army officer, Chapman, by name.[2] Hon. Nestor Armijo, of Las Cruces, told me of having passed down the valley into Mexico in that year, and saw the men at work. In 1849 he returned to his home in the northern end of the Territory, and states that there were houses and people living in them.

The name, Las Cruces, comes from the Spanish, 'The Crosses'; it was given to the settlement because of fearful tragedy which occurred years before, and to the Hon. S.G. Bean I am indebted for the following description.

In 1840, a party of forty Mexicans were on a journey from New Mexico to the State of Chihuahua with a train of pack-mules on a trading expedition, as it was the custom every year to make these trips for the purpose of exchanging commodities.

At the point where the town of Las Cruces now stands there was a fearful mesquite jungle; (more probably toward the north end of town, near the present site of the Alameda Sanitarium, and Fletcher's old ranch)[3] *where the Indians, who held high carnival in the wilderness of this valley, waited the coming of the unsuspecting party. They made the onslaught from ambush, and it was a 'Custer Massacre', as not one of the forty Mexicans were left to tell the bloody tale.*

At that time there were no telegraph lines to wire the appalling news to kindred and friends, but they received notice by some means, and kind friends came and paid their last respects to the dead. Every spot of ground was marked where each bloody corpse was found by two boards nailed as the symbols of the holy cross. These crosses were standing here when I first came to the Territory in 1846.

Today a huge black cross stands in the yard of St. Genevieve's Catholic church in memory of that black deed; an older one just like it used to stand in front of the church, but it was taken up and a new cross on the east side was erected in place of the old decaying one. Two other mute memorials, two semi-cylinder shaped masonry mounts, are to be found half hidden among the tall mesquite bushes near some small scattering Mexican houses, about a block and a half north of St. Genevieve's church.

Not long after Las Cruces was settled, a band of Pueblo Indians from Juárez came and made their home in the town. Since the early '50s these Indians have had their regular rabbit hunts, dances before the church, and illuminations upon the mountains and in town two weeks before Christmas and on Christmas eve.[4] Las Cruces has always contained the largest percentage of people of any town in the valley, while the Mexican population is greatly mixed with this Pueblo blood.

In studying over the church records, the first entry was a baptism, one Manuel Chavez, May 16th, 1859. The Father informed me that the first books were lost in a fire years ago, and that they were very poor and primitive because the priests only came periodically as they traveled around in the diocese.[5]

The Mesilla Valley furnished wheat and grain for Ft. Fillmore and Arizona as well, so that very early in the history of this town, two mills were set in operation. The one at the north end of town, owned now by Don Barbaro Lucero, was built by Pedro Diaz; its next owners were Telles and Ochoa; next Carbonier, and about fourteen years ago it went to the present owner; the one on the south side now owned by Mr. [Jacob] Schaublin was first in the possession of Mr. [Henry] Lesinsky, from whom it passed into the hands of Grangene [Numa Grandjean].[6]

The oldest buildings in Las Cruces are upon Main Street; night watchmen were necessary as late as '68, so Hon. Numa Reymond told me.

Mrs. M.B. Aguirre of Phoenix, Ariz., who was one of the early white women in Las Cruces, read a paper on her life in the valley before the Federation of Women's Clubs of Arizona at Phoenix, November 23rd, 1901; the lady gave me the liberty of using the following extract;

I made my first trip 'across the plains' in the fall of 1863 (Sept.); there were ten mule wagons and four ambulances, which composed 'the train.' The ambulances used then for crossing the plains, or any long overland journey, were marvels of comfort—we tho't—being arranged so the seats could be spread out for sleeping, as are the Pullman sleepers of today. There were toilet arrangements of all kinds under the back seats and in pockets in the doors. There were places for clothes and sewing boxes. It looked on the outside like a rather long carriage and the doors opened on the sides and glasses in them like hacks have. They cost between five and six hundred dollars. We traveled very slowly, never making more than twenty miles a day, which was the fastest time made. But we seldom made more than fifteen miles. The day's journeys were made to reach certain well known watering places, which were mostly only deep holes, made by the rains. The 'plains' I speak of are the prairie lands, five hundred miles of rolling, grassy land that looks as boundless as the sea; and when the wind blows over the tall grass it looks like the waves of the ocean,—those long smooth green waves we see in shallow water. We saw herds of Buffalo like we see herds of cattle on Arizona ranches. Our fresh meat was furnished by these herds, by the hunters of the party, and was hunted on horse back. We saw droves of antelope and they too were made to supply us with fresh meat. Can you imagine yourselves going two months over a journey that now adays is made in two days? It took us two months to go from Kansas City to Santa Fé, New Mexico, and our journey was not yet over, we still had nearly four hundred miles to travel. We lost count of time. It was the true 'Dolce por nienta.'

Arizona then was part of New Mexico, and almost an unknown part. The Federal Government was established in Arizona that year (1863), making it an independent territory and the Governor (Goodwin) and his officers came across the plains as we came, some of the party traveling with our train. They went on to Prescott and we went to Las Cruces, New Mexico; it was wonderfully interesting in those times. It always reminded me of Bible lands, and the customs were certainly of Bible times. For instance they plowed with a steel or iron shod pointed stick, the oxen were tied by the horns (they always used oxen). The furrows were deepened by one yoke of oxen following the other to the number of twelve in the same furrow till the required depth was reached. The strongest man and oxen led the furrow. Do you remember an expression in the Bible where it says 'And he (Jacob) led the furrow?' I never knew what that meant till I saw that long line of plows following each other in the same furrow. There were no board floors or unnecessary wood work. The rafters of *the house were unhewn logs; the windows had wooden bars up and down and shutters outside rough hewn; there were no glass windows. The windows had wooden bars and shutters, and some small openings were filled with isin-glass. I had the first glass window of any size in Las Cruces. The panes were very small and there were a great many to each sash and the window cost $60.00. It was the comfort of my life and the admiration of the town. The natives would stand two rows deep outside looking in at me sitting on the broad adobe window sill. Then the babies were not dressed as they are now. They were wrapped in swaddling clothes a succession of wide and narrow bands, with a beautiful embroidered or drawnworked one out side. Their little hands and arms were strapped tight down with the bands. **** Furniture was home made and very scarce and high. Books were impossible unless we had brought them with us. Newspapers and letters came once a month in winter and every two weeks in summer. In telling about part of the New Mexico that was settled, but in our beloved Arizona, there was not even the few comforts I speak of. And now the old order has changed giving place to new, and God has revealed himself to us in many ways.*

The town, right on the booming river, and most favorable for agricultural pursuits, grew rapidly. Although La Mesilla for many, many years was heavily populated, with the advent of the Santa Fé Railroad in 1881, Las Cruces ran far ahead and is so today.

The latitude of the town is 32° 19' north; its population according to the last census is 3,500.

Picacho. The little town of Picacho, over upon the mountain of that name, now haunted by coyotes, was built about 1855. With the removal of the Butterfield stage it went down, and years ago every one left because of the scarcity of water in the river.

The Mesilla Valley had its first newspaper in 1860, *The Mesilla News* which was run [published] for two years.

In 1869 a struggling young foreigner started the first express company down through the valley. This man became the wealthiest, and one of the most prominent men in the valley, and a loss was felt when he recently closed his business here, and left for his home in Switzerland; his name was Numa Reymond.

Looking east from Griggs Street in Las Cruces, 1892.
Courtesy: Rio Grande Historical Collections, New Mexico State University.

The Academy of Visitation, Sisters of Loretto, was established in Las Cruces in January, 1870.[7] There were four sisters: Sister Rosan was the first Mother Superior; these brave women were brought across the plains by Bishop J.B. Salpointe.[8] There was a smaller convent, tho of a different order, in La Mesilla. It was established early in the history of that town.

Twice have small denominational schools been started here, and both have been abandoned.

The U.S. Land Office was established in late 1876 at La Mesilla, with its first officials—Messrs. [George D.] Bowman and S[amuel] W. Sherfey.

In 1886 the Las Cruces College was incorporated. The incorporators were John R. McFie, Hiram Hadley, S[imon] B. Newcomb, George D. Bowman and James R. Waddill. The first Board of Trustees were Pres. John R. McFie, Vice-Pres. W[illiam] L. Rynerson, Sec. James R. Waddill, Treas. Numa Reymond, Jacob Schaublin, and J.B. Joblin. Hiram Hadley, who has ever since been connected in the highest positions with the institution, was chosen the first president.

The first enrollment was forty.

By act of the legislature of 1888 and 1889, the Agricultural College was located at Las Cruces, and the Las Cruces College became the Agricultural College, with the following constituting the first Board of Regents, John R. McFie, President; William L. Rynerson, Sec. and Treas.; Robert Black, J[ames] A. Whitmore and Numa Reymond.

Another building was rented, a building for higher grades, and entered it on January 21, 1890. In the meantime, the present main building was going up and was occupied in the spring of that same year. Since then four new buildings have been up, and wonderful improvement of farm and department equipment has taken place.

Shalam. One of the interesting things to relate concerning the valley is the history of the colony, situated a mile west of Doña Ana, called Shalam.[9]

The colony was formed in response to a book entitled *Oahspe—* a historical, socialistic, and religious work written by Dr. J[ohn] B. Newbrough of New York. The book was written in 1883, and by the fall of 1884 a small band of people came to the Mesilla Valley, and, purchasing a vast tract of land from John Barncastle of Doña Ana, settled upon it.

The founders and trustees of this socialistic colony were Dr. J.B. Newbrough and Mr. A[ndrew] M. Howland of Boston.

There was large capital behind the colony; the land was some of the best in the valley, fine buildings with all modern conveniences were put up and every industry started that was necessary to make the place self-supporting.

As provided for by their creed, Dr. Newbrough went out to the great cities to bring to Shalam orphans and castaways. The first children came from New Orleans, at different dates, and from many of the large cities, others were taken into the colony.

In 1891, Dr. Newbrough died.

Ten years later the place disbanded. After having been carried thru a great law suit, the property went to Mr. A.M. Howland, who, with his family, has lived there ever since.

The world is not "sufficiently sickened of miserable poverty for the many and vast untold millions for the few"—and Shalam with its principal of Equality and Co-operation was a failure.

FORTS

From the entrace of Doniphan's army into the Mesilla Valley up to the year 1891, except from January 1863 to May 1865, there have been troops garrisoned here.

At first they were cavalry-dragoons, but later infantry was stationed here under Capt. [Oliver L.] Shephard. These troops were stationed right in the town of Doña Ana, and, as might be expected it proved unsatisfactory, for the soldiers became demoralized, and the citizens objected to them. I have been unable to find out reliably as to whether or not there was any official document requesting the government to remove the soldiers; anyway, it was done in September, 1851. The site of the new fort [Fort Fillmore] was chosen upon the Bracito Grant; and the government leased a tract one mile square, for twenty years from Mr. Stephenson, who owned the part of the grant upon which the site was, for $200,000.00.[10] The soldiers lived in tents,

46

and were paid extra for their services in building the Fort. This was destined to play a most important part in the history of the South West, for it was the frontier post and the most important strategic point on the border.

The troops that went into the completed post on September 23rd, 1851, were Company H, 1st Dragoons, and Companies E and F, 3rd Infantry. The fort received its name as an honor to President Millard Fillmore, who was then serving his term in the White House. The building of this fort was really the building of La Mesilla, for it was nearer than either Doña Ana or Las Cruces, and the troops demanded much produce in the way of food, grain and hay.

Ft. Fillmore was abandoned by the Union forces on July 25th, 1861, and fell into the hands of the Confederates. It was re-occupied by the U.S. troops from August 11th, 1862 to November 13th, 1862; then in January 1863, the buildings were dismantled for use at other posts.

The ruins of Ft. Fillmore come in sight after a seven mile ride down our College road. The buildings are half way up the sand bluffs. To one who is sight-seeing, the location instantly strikes one as not being a good one, because an attack could easily be made upon three sides from above, and, the approach of the enemy almost completely hidden. Probably had this been different, the history of the fort would have been other than it is.

Ft. Selden, situated near Doña Ana was established May 8th, 1865; it was named in honor of the Memory of Col. Henry Selden, 1st New Mexico Infantry, and Major, 13th Infantry, who died February 2nd, of the same year. Its first occupants were Company M, 1st Cavalry [California], and Company C, 1st Veteran [Volunteer, New Mexico] Infantry, under the command of Capt. James H. Whitlock of the latter regiment.[11]

It was occupied until March 11th, 1877, when the troops were withdrawn and sent to Fort Craig, N.M.; the post was abandoned August 8th, 1878, and the buildings dismantled. It was again occupied December 25th, 1880, by Troop M, 9th Cavalry, under the command of Capt. Louis H. Rucker of the 9th Cavalry. Six months later, July 12th, 1881, these troops were followed by Company K, 15th Infantry. The post was finally abandoned January 22nd, 1891, and the Mesilla Valley has had no regular troops since that date.

THE RIVER

The Rio Bravo del Norte was the old Spanish [name] for the poor excuse of a river we now call the Rio Grande. Who, learning first of this river from the maps does not imagine it a great noble stream, and very important? It has been important, however, for it was never dry the three summer months early in the history of our valley, and over its shifting, restless banks has hung national arbitration more than once. Hon. Horace Stephenson remembers knowing of the river being completely dry in 1837; all the people gathered to see this sight, and the children to play in its dry sands. Never-the-less the other times the water came in terrible floods; banks could scarcely check the volume of water, and everything had to be ferried across almost the year around. At several places down the valley there were ferry stations, and many of the people owned private boats.

The course of the river was that of a decided bend cut away from the hills, beginning north about opposite Doña Ana. Old maps and plats show that the bed has meandered over the bottoms, but the only accurate data I could get was its bed as seen plainly near the A.T. and S.F. rail road track, which crosses it where now lie the Nicols, and the Kezer, ranches, on behind the court house, and down the valley until it is crossed by the college avenue, just at the entrance of the college grounds; then on down the valley until it again slopes into the present channel a few miles below us.

The following are the facts agreed upon by my pioneer informants: the great Mesilla ditch head tapping the river had weakened its bank on the west side, and each spring when the freshets of water came from the melting ice at the north, the natives had to turn out in great numbers to stand guard over the ditch head, and strengthen the bank the best they could.

When the Rebellion came to occupy the people with other dangers, the river was uncared for as in former years, and some time one May night the great spring rise broke the limits and flooded the country. This went on for two or three years, each year water came over and, after lying, became unhealthful, so causing the dreadful epidemic of chills and fever and malaria for which the valley was noted for years, even yet, unfortunately, though the cause and effect have been eradicated these many years.

In the spring rise of 1865, the volume of water was so enormous that it took everything before it, and made a mad dash down the valley along the hills on the west—a short cut, which left the town of La Mesilla high and dry upon the opposite bank about a mile away. The valley is described as one vast sheet of water from the edge of Las Cruces to the hills on the west, with the site of La Mesilla a strip of island. It is said that for years the river actually ran into this bend, keeping the water high and almost deadly to inhabitants. However a movement of the people, headed by the *Mayor-Domo*, dammed up the mouth, and in a few years the stagnant water had evaporated, and people began to take up their residence in the valley and farm lands upon the rich deposit area of the former river bed.

During the war times the road to La Mesilla from El Paso led up over Lava Mesa because the water lay in vast connected lagoons in the bottoms, where the road had formerly been.

In 1884-85 the river again caused a great deal of trouble in the country below. Big floods descended and the waters covered miles upon miles of hitherto high and dry land. Both Chamberino and La Union had to be deserted entirely and new settlements made upon the hills, while the former settlement called Los Amoles was given to the raging waters, and is only marked today by a lonely tree or so, or a solitary stump where a bird may balance.

In connection with the river, it will be remembered the enthusiasm created by the prospect of the famous Elephant Butte Dam in the 90s. In 1893 the Rio Grande Dam and Irrigation Company was incorporated under the laws of New Mexico; later a company was formed in England. Col. W.J. Engledue, R.E., an authority on irrigation engineering, for many years identified with the Imperial Irrigation Works in India, visited the Rio Grande Valley on behalf of the English investors and reported most favorably. A large colonization scheme went through, and brought about twenty-five people to the valley as settlers. Work on the proposed dams and canals was begun in 1896, and continued until 1897. The general plan was to construct a huge dam at Elephant Butte, making this point the largest storage reservoir in the world. There were to be smaller dams, and together with canals, it will bring, when finally finished, under cultivation hundreds of thousands of acres, making our valley the garden spot of the world. In

1897, the United States brought suit to enjoin the Company from building its dam; work stopped immediately and all the money sunk, —about $250,000—was left exposed to destruction by heavy flows of water.

The grounds for the suit were; that the Rio Grande was a navigable stream, the utter absurdity of which is plain to everyone who has seen it, and it is positively unnavigable for fully nine hundred miles below El Paso,—that by virtue of the fact that Mexico never reserved the right to any portion of the waters of the Rio Grande flowing through the United States in her treaties with the United States, shows that she lost the rights. This is confidently and conclusively contended by lawyers in the employ of the Company; but the true secret of the attack upon the Elephant Butte Dam seems to be an International Dam in the extreme lower edge of the Mesilla Valley near El Paso. The case has been dragged from the lowest court to the highest then back, and litigation is not ended yet.[12]

Hon. M[iguel] A. Otero, Gov. of New Mexico, in his Annual Report of 1899 to the Secretary of Interior, says; *"The greatest setback this section has ever had was that resulting from the stopping of work on what is familiarly known as the Elephant Butte Dam."*[13]

WAR OF THE REBELLION
1861-1862

The Mesilla Valley had its full share of the Rebellion. The Indians, always more or less bad, became very bold and active, in their treachery and murder. Among the population were sympathizers of both North and South; the Mexican people leaned toward the Union— Bancroft states the opposite—and the Union soldiers were in possession of Ft. Fillmore on the Bracito.[14] Feeling was strong and bitter, and over the confiscation of property and wealth that changed hands following the armies, some awful tragedies resulted. June 11th, 1861, Col. E.R.S. Canby, 19th U.S. Infantry, was placed in general charge of affairs in the Department of New Mexico with headquarters at Santa Fé; and July 3rd, 1861, New Mexico was embraced in the Western Department.[15]

50

At this time the headquarters of the Southern District of New Mexico was at Ft. Fillmore, and it was represented by Maj. Isaac Lynde of the 7th Infantry, also commander of that post. On July 8th, Brig. Gen. Henry H. Sibley of the Confederate Army was ordered to Texas to expel the Union forces from there and New Mexico.

On July 18th, Capt. J.H. Potter, 7th Infantry, in charge of two companies of infantry, was sent to occupy Santo Tomás, on the river, because it commanded the road from El Paso to La Mesilla, over which the Confederates were passing constantly. At this time all wagons were stopped and searched for ammunition from Texas passing up. The river was so uncertain a factor that at that time the road led away up over the *Mal Pais* as the Mexicans call the lava mesa from that worn little volcanic cone plainly seen on the *Lomas* (hills) to the southwest.

Lieut. Col. John R. Baylor assumed command at Ft. Bliss, Texas. On the night of July 23rd, he, with a force of 258 Texan Rangers, marched up the Rio Grande, arriving at La Mesilla on the afternoon of the 25th. Later in the afternoon, about four or five o'clock, Maj. Isaac Lynde forded the river from Ft. Fillmore and made a poor attack upon the troops in La Mesilla.

REPORT OF MAJ. ISAAC LYNDE TO DEPARTMENT HEADQUARTERS, SANTA FÉ, N.M.

Hdqrs., Southern District, New Mexico
Fort Fillmore, N.Mex., July 26, 1861

Sir: I have the honor to report that on the night of the 24th inst. a deserter from the Texas troops was brought in by our picket, and he informed me that a large body of mounted men, between 300 and 400, under the command of Lieutenant Colonel Baylor, Texas troops, were moving up the river, and that he left them at Willow Bar, about 12 miles below the post. Presuming their object to be an attack on the post, I immediately ordered in the two companies of the Seventh Infantry from San Tomas, and kept the garrison under arms after daylight, when mounted parties were sent out to reconnoiter. In the mean time, the enemy passed up the opposite side of the river through the town of San Tomas, where they captured 7 of the men of my command left behind by the battalion of the Seventh Infantry in the hurry of departure. After extracting from them what information they could in reference to the probable time of the arrival of the troops of Forts Breckenridge and Buchanan, they were released, and joined the post. All property, public and private, belonging to the command was seized and carried off or destroyed.

About 4,30 o'clock p.m. yesterday I moved in the direction of the town of Mesilla, where the Texas troops then were, six companies of the Seventh Infantry, one acting as artillery, with the howitzer battery of the post and two companies of rifles ...

About 2 miles from Mesilla, I sent Lieutenant Brooks, Seventh Infantry, A.A.A.C., forward with a white flag to demand the surrender of the town. He was met by Maj. Waller and Col. Herbert on the part of the Texans, who replied that if I wanted the town I must come and take it. I moved the battery forward and fired two shells at long range, but they burst in the air short of the object. The command continued to advance slowly towards the outskirts of the town, while the battery, which had to be moved by hand, was working through the heavy sand. From a corn field and house on the right, we received a heavy fire of musketry, wounding 2 officers and 4 men and killing 3 men. As night was coming on, and the fields and houses on both sides of the road were filled with men, and the howitzers useless, except as a field battery, owing to the difficulty of moving through the sand, I decided to withdraw my forces and return to my post. The march back was uninterrupted, and to-day I am fortifying with sand bags, &c. in anticipation of an attack. I have sent express instructions to Captain Gibbs, directing him to return to Fort Craig with his command, as he cannot join this post now. They have possession of the road above. Orders will be sent, if possible, to the commanders of the troops from Forts Breckenridge and Buchanan to take the nearest route to Fort Craig from a point where the orders reach them.

A reinforcement of 100 men joined the Texans from Fort Bliss last night. Their force at present, with the addition of the citizens of Mesilla, is nearly 700 men. I am hourly expecting an attack. The loss of the enemy is reported 11 killed and wounded. Part of their horses were stampeded by one of our shells.

I am, sir, very respectfully, your obedient servant,

I. Lynde,
Major, Seventh Infantry, Commanding

Fort Craig, N. Mex., August 7th, 1861
Sir: On the 26th of July, I had the honor to report the fact of an unsuccessful attempt to dislodge the Texan troops from the town of Mesilla, since which events of the greatest consequence to my command have occurred. They are now prisoners of war.

On that day I had reliable information that the enemy would in the course of the night receive a battery of artillery, and if I moved to intercept it with a sufficient force for the purpose they were ready to attack the fort in my absence, and, as I have previously reported, the fort is indefensible against artillery, being perfectly commanded by sand hills for at least half the circle, and the only supply of water at a distance of one and a half miles. Other officers, with myself, became convinced that we must eventually be compelled to surrender if we remained in the fort, and that our only hope of saving the command from capture was in reaching some other military post. I therefore ordered the fort to be evacuated, and such public property as could not be transported with the limited means at the post to be destroyed as far as time would allow, and at 1 o'clock a.m. on the 27th of July, I took up the line of march for Fort Stanton, which was believed to be the most practicable point to reach, and was reported to be threatened by the enemy. I had no personal knowledge of the road, but it was reported to me that the first day's march would be 20 miles to Saint Augustine Springs, where there would be abundance of water for all the command.[16]

Until daylight the command advanced without difficulty, but when the sun rose the day became intensely hot, and soon after the men and teams began to show signs of fatigue, and I found that the distance was greater than represented. About 6 miles before reaching the Springs, commences a short ascent to a pass in the Organ Mountains, and here the men and teams suffered severely with the intense heat and want of water, many men falling and unable to proceed.

Up to this time there was no indication of pursuit. I now determined to push forward with the mounted forces to the Springs, and return with water for the suffering force in the rear. When I had nearly reached the Springs word was brought to me that a mounted force was approaching our rear; but it was believed to be Captain Gibbs, R.M.R., with his command, and soon after that supposition was confirmed by another express.

Upon reaching the Springs I found the supply of water so small as to be insufficient for my command. After procuring all the water that could be transported by the men with me I started back to the main body. After riding some distance I became so exhausted that I could not sit my horse, and the command proceeded without me, under the command of Lieutenant Cressey, R.M.R., and I returned to the Springs. Soon after it was reported to me that a part of the teams had given out and could not be brought up, and that a large number of the infantry had become totally overpowered with the intense heat. At this time an express from Captain Gibbs reported that eight companies of mounted men, supported by artillery and a large force of infantry, were approaching our rear guard. I had the 'Call to Arms' sounded, and found that I could not bring more than 100 men of the infantry battalion on parade. Captain Gibbs, with a mounted force, now rode into camp, and stated to me that eight companies of mounted Texans (supported by a regiment of infantry, more or less) were approaching; that they had driven on or captured our rear guard (composed of three companies of infantry) and the men that had given out in the rear. Three of the four mountain howitzers that we had with us were with the wagons in the rear and were captured. They were guarded by one company of infantry, acting as artillery. Captain Gibbs also reported that his company, men and horses, had been without water for twenty-four hours.

Under the circumstances, I considered our case hopeless; that it was worse than useless to resist; that honor did not demand the sacrifice of blood after the terrible suffering that our troops had already undergone, and when that sacrifice would be useless. A body of mounted Texans followed Captain Gibbs to the vicinity of the camp, when a parley was held, and I surrendered my command to Lieutenant Colonel Baylor of the C.S. Army.

54

The strength of my command at the time of surrender was, Mounted Rifles, 95 rank and file, and 2 officers. The infantry I have not the means of stating the exact number, but there were seven companies of the Seventh Infantry with 8 officers present. Since I have been at Fort Fillmore my position has been of extreme embarrassment. Surrounded by open or secret enemies, no reliable information could be obtained, and disaffection prevailing, even in my own command, to what extent it was impossible to ascertain, but much increased, undoubtedly, by the conduct of the officers who left their post without authority. My position has been one of great difficulty, and has ended in the misfortune of surrendering my command to the enemy. The Texan troops acted with great kindness to our men, exerting themselves in carrying water to the famishing ones in the rear; yet it was two days before the infantry could move from camp, and then only with the assistance of their captors. The officers and men who chose to give their parole were released at Las Cruces, N. Mex...

Very respectfully your obedient servant,

I. Lynde,

Major, Seventh Infantry[17]

Major Lynde, with three companies of the regiment mounted rifles, arrived, on parole, at Fort Craig, on the sixth of August, 1861.

A recapitulation of the troops surrendered at San Augustine on July 27th, 1861, is as follows:

RELEASED ON PAROLE: 1 major, 2 assistant surgeons, 2 captains, 5 first lieutenants, 1 second lieutenant: total commissioned, 11. 1 sergeant-major, 1 quartermaster-sergeant, 1 principal musician, 23 sergeants, 22 corporals, 7 musicians, 344 privates: total enlisted, 399. Aggregate, 410.

In confinement as prisoners of war: 1 sergeant, 15 privates: total, 16.

Deserted to enemy; 1 hospital steward, 1 sergeant, 24 privates: total, 26.

Available for service, not paroled: 2 sergeants, 3 corporals, 35 privates: total 40.

J.H. POTTER,

Captain, Seventh Infantry, Commanding.[18]

The above shows Maj. Lynde's side of the affair, and tho he was bitterly criticized and finally dismissed from the army, consideration should be shown a man so pressed by enemies whom he thought were friends. In his book, *40 Years at El Paso*, Hon. W.W. Mills states,

He was not treacherous, he was weak, and he was deceived to his ruin and disgrace of his flag. I have never doubted that had he been properly supported and encouraged the result would have been different. Of his subalterns, some resigned, some joined the enemy, and some went into the recruiting and quartermaster's service, none, so far as I know, except McNally ever did much fighting. I do not censure all of them, but I thought, and still think, that there should have been one among them who would have assumed command, arrested Lynde, and won a colonel's eagles.[19]

In Col. Baylor's report he states,

Major Lynde's command was composed of eight companies of infantry and four of cavalry, with four pieces of artillery, the whole numbering nearly 700 men. My own forces at the surrender was less than 200. I regret to report that the regimental colors were burned by the enemy to avoid surrendering them.[20]

After getting rid of the prisoners, for his force was too weak to hold them, Baylor selected a strong position near the village of Picacho to wait the arrival of Capt. Moore who was enroute from Ft. Buchanan to Ft. Fillmore with 250 men. Here he was joined by Brig. Gen. A[lbert] S[idney] Johnston with a party of officers of the U.S. Army, who had resigned and were bound for Richmond, Va.; also a party of Californians, under Capt. Alonzo Ridley. Being a superior officer, Gen. Johnston accepted the command of affairs and remained until his services were no longer necessary.

Capt. Moore received a dispatch from Ft. Craig informing him of the surrender of Maj. Lynde's command and ordering him to burn supplies, and make his escape to that place, avoid running into ambush. The jaded condition of Col. Baylor's horses prevented him from capturing the retreating unionists.

On August 1st, 1861, Col. Baylor issued a proclamation to the people taking formal possession in the name of the Confederate States and announcing himself Governor. The whole of the proclamation is given under the head of 'Military and Territorial Government.' The taking and giving up of Ft. Stanton with minor engagements near Ft. Craig which was the strongest point in Southern New Mexico, together with minor engagements and terrible Indian troubles occupied the attention of the Confederates, and in a letter Col. Baylor said he would make no move toward the enemy until the arrival of Gen. Sibley.

The following is an extract from Col. Canby to the War Department, December 8th, 1861.

The Confederate force in the Mesilla Valley is about 800 men of their regular troops and from 200 to 400 men organized from the floating population of the Mesilla. These troops are well armed and cavalry well mounted, but they are indifferently clothed and subsisted. They have fifteen pieces of artillery, of which two are said to be heavy —probably 18 pounders—four mountain howitzers and the remainder field pieces, 6 pounder guns, and 12 pounder howitzers. They have fallen back from their advanced position at Robledo and are now at or near Mesilla.[21]

Later in December, Brig. Gen. H.H. Sibley and army came to the Territory and issued a proclamation on December 20th, 1861, also given under the heading of 'Military and Territorial Government,' but left Col. Baylor to continue the full exercise of the functions of his office of civil and military governor.

In February 1862, Sibley marched up through Mesilla and Ft. Thorn. During the events that followed in the spring, when [with] the battle of Valverde and the taking possession of Santa Fé, while Gen. Canby and Col. Roberts were in strength at Ft. Craig, nothing of great interest happened in the Mesilla Valley.

Colorado troops saved the day for New Mexico, and sent the Texans under Sibley back down through the Mesilla Valley to Ft. Bliss, in the first part of May, 1862.

Troops still remained in the valley until early in July, when the famous California Volunteers reached the Rio Grande. It has been said that in killed, wounded, prisoners, and stragglers, this Confederate army had left nearly half their original force—3800 men and 327 wagons—in New Mexico.[22]

Ft. Fillmore was re-occupied on August 11th by Unionists, and in January of the following year was dismantled for use of other posts. Thus was the end of the rebellion in Mesilla Valley.

Major Isaac Lynde was dropped from Army rolls from November 25th, 1861, to November 27th, 1866; he was reinstated, as Major of the 18th Infantry, to date from July 28th, 1866. He was retired from active service on the date of his reappointment, November 27th, 1866.[23]

ORGAN MINES

The Organ mines are on what is known as the 'Big Contact,' which extends along the base of the foothills of the Organ Range on the west side and from below the Modoc at the south end to the Little Buck on the north—a distance of fifteen miles. The trend of the Contact is northeast, [and dips] off [to the] north and northwest.[24]

Modoc Mine: Located in 1880 by James Rynerson, now owned by the Modoc Mining Co.—Harold Crane Sons—with Frank Larchen, Superintendent; capital about $1,000,000; cost of plant, dry concentrator, $125,000; amount of work done, 2000 to 3500 feet; large bodies of lead ore carrying some silver.[25]

Torpedo Mine: Located early in the '90s by Foy Bros. and Redding. It is now owned by the Torpedo Mining Co., having been bought by the Company in 1899; George E. Fitzgerald, Superintendent; capital $1,000,000; cost of plant, steam hoist boilers, etc., $25,000. Thousands of tons of copper ore have been taken out in the last three years and shipped via Santa Fe Railroad at Las Cruces to El Paso smelter. 1,000 feet of shaft; 4,000 feet in levels and drifts. New working shaft 300 feet now flooded.[26]

The Stephenson, now known as the Bennett-Stephenson, was the first mine discovered in Doña Ana County. It was brought to light by prospectors in the employ of Hon. Hugh Stephenson, who were sent out to search the Organs from Franklin, at El Paso, to San Augustine Pass, for the traditional 'Padre Mine.' This was in 1851. Mr. Stephenson built a smelter near what is now known as the Ascarate Ranch [near Ft. Fillmore], and worked the lead until the later part of 1858. The owner extracted something over $70,000 of silver during that time. The mine was called the 'Santo Domingo' but became the Stephenson when sold, in the latter part of 1858, to Major John T. Sprague, then stationed at Fort Fillmore. Some years ago the property was consolidated with the Bennett property, and the two go under the title given in the first line of this topic.[27]

Bennett Mine: Located November 15th, 1880, by Col. J[oseph] F. Bennett, now owned by the Stephenson-Bennett Consolidated Mining Co. Cost of plant, concentrator and four-inch pipe line 1 3/4 miles in length, from Memphis shaft, $50,000. W.H. Skidmore states that not less than 50,000 tons of ore have been taken out of the mine and shipped by wagon to Las Cruces and thence to Pueblo and El Paso smelters. Ore is argentiferous galena.[28]

Memphis Mine: Located in 1861 by Col. O'Bannon, now owned by the Stephenson-Bennett Consolidated Mining Co. Was worked during the early '80s by John Cunningham and others under the superintendence of W.J. Joblin. Took out in surface workings considerable high grade copper ore which was smelted on the ground, two and one-half carloads of copper bullion was shipped; at this time much work was also done in development among which was a working shaft 170 feet in depth and in a level near the bottom of this shaft there is said to be a six-foot breadth of ore that runs 32 ozs. silver, 11 ozs. copper, and $4.00 gold, now under water. There is a future to this mine under good management.[29]

Excelsior Mine was also located in the early '80s by W. Daniels, H. Simpson and others. Now owned by Capt. Dunbar and W.R. McCormick. It has been worked for years at a profit and its ore—

high grade copper—shipped by wagon and railroad to El Paso, Texas. A gasoline engine hoist, blacksmith shop, three snug cottages are the only surface improvements. This mine bears a good reputation among the mining men.[30]

<u>Little Buck Mine</u>, located in 1881 by G.J. Greathouse, S.N. Perkins and Duncan McCowan. Very little work has been done on this mine over assessments for a number of years, although in the past, Greathouse, McCowan, Hughes, and others realized small fortunes in working the property.[31]

Last year Prof. A. Goss, Chemist at the New Mexico College of Agriculture and Mechanic Arts, Mesilla Park, N.M., leased the property during his vacation and took out a few thousand dollars. He carefully prospected the vein and made numerous assays, and was rewarded by the discovery of inch gold on first assay. On one ton of this he realized, after all freight and mailing charges had been deducted, $1,023.00, gold. Professor Goss also shipped several tons of silver ore, two tons of this sampled at the mine 1,281 ounces in silver, some gold, which at 50 cents per ounce was worth or would net after smelter and freight charges were deducted about $600.00 per ton.

Freight (wagon) from Modoc and other mines to the A.T. and S. F.R.R. Depot $2.50 to $4.00 per ton. Railroad freight to smelter, El Paso, in carload lots $1.50 per ton. Thousands of tons of ore from Organ camp have been shipped to Pueblo at $5.00 per ton and upwards.[32]

Notes:

[1] T. Frank White's Ranch was at Frontera. Garcia's ranch was in the Bracito Grant. Fletcher's ranch house was on the present day Three Crosses Avenue near Alameda Blvd. *J.T.B.*

[2] Most other sources give the credit for surveying Las Cruces to 2nd Lt. Delos Bennet Sacket. According to the *Rio Grande Republican* (Las Cruces, N.M.), April 18, 1885, Don Pablo Melendres asked Lt. Sacket to lay out the town in the spring of 1849, which he did with the help of five men, including George Ackenback. *J.T.B.*

60

[3] The Alameda Sanitarium was probably the old Alameda Resort Ranch, located near the intersection of present day (1998) Townsend Terrace and Alameda Blvd. Not far away was the Fletcher house on Three Crosses Ave. *J.T.B.*

[4] For more on these Indians and settlers, see Patrick H. Beckett and Terry L. Corbett, *Tortugas* (Las Cruces: Coas Publishing and Research, 1990). *J.T.B.*

[5] See Rosemary Buchanan, *The First 100 Years: St. Genevieve's Parish, 1859-1959* (Las Cruces: Bronson Printing Co., 1961). *J.T.B.*

[6] The Lucero Mill was located on the acequia at the end of Church St., between First and Oregon. That is about where the Fire Station and Police Headquarters buildings are in 1998. The Las Cruces Flour Mill, owned by Jacob Schaublin, was south of the convent and west of the acequia. El Molino Blvd. is probably the present day location. These locations are based on the 1913 Sanborn map of Las Cruces in the Special Collections of the New Mexico State University Library. *J.T.B.*

[7] The Academy faced East Lohman Avenue at Main Street, the present site of the Loretto Towne Center. *J.T.B.*

[8] The Mother Superior was Mother Rosanna Dant. See Wendy C. Simpson, "The Sisters of Loretto in Las Cruces: The Education of a Frontier Community, 1870-1943," *La Crónica de Nuevo México*, 47: pp. 3-6 (May 1998). *J.T.B.*

[9] For more on Shalam Colony, see Lee Priestley, *Shalam: Utopia on the Rio Grande, 1881-1907* (El Paso: The University of Texas at El Paso Press, 1988): and Elinore W. Wiley, *Inside the Shalam Colony* (Los Alamos, New Mexico: The Document Shop, 1991). *J.T.B.*

[10] More likely the rent was 1 penny per year. See Corinne C. Mozer, "A Brief History of Fort Fillmore, 1851-1862," *El Palacio*, 74: 6, note 3. This issue of *El Palacio* (Summer, 1967) contains several fine articles on Fort Fillmore. *J.T.B.*

[11] The site of Ft. Selden was previously occupied by the village of Robledo, settled in 1843. *L.L.B.* A good history of Ft. Selden is Allan J. Holmes, "Fort Selden, 1965-1891: The Birth, Life, and Death of a Southwestern Fort," unpublished master's thesis, New Mexico State University, 1990. *J.T.B.*

[12] *Report of the Governor of New Mexico to the Secretary of the Interior, 1899* (Washington: Government Printing Office, 1899), p. 304. This *Report* can be found in "The Territorial Archives of New Mexico," (microform), roll 148. *J.T.B.*

[13] *Ibid.*, p. 303.

[14] Bancroft also points out on p. 684 that most New Mexicans, including the Mexicans were loyal to the Union. *J.T.B.*

[15] My data for the campaign of 1861 and 1862, called by Hon. W.W. Mills the "Canby-Sibley" portion of the Rebellion, is taken from *The War of Rebellion*, Series I, Volume IV: 2-90; Volume IX: 481-545, 549-607; Bancroft, *History of Arizona and New Mexico*; and data from the Adjut. Gen. of U.S. Army, throught [*sic*] correspondence. In justice to one long since passed away, I have taken whole letters from the records. *M.E.M.*

[16] Now known as Aguirre Springs, on the east side of the Organ Mountains. Mozer, "History of Fort Fillmore," p. 13. *J.T.B.*

[17] *The War of the Rebellion*, IV: 4-7.

[18] *The War of the Rebellion*, IV: 15.

[19] Mills, *Forty Years at El Paso*, p. 53.

[20] Report of Lieutenant Colonel John R. Baylor, September 21, 1861, *The War of Rebellion*, IV: 19.

[21] *The War of Rebellion*, IV: 79.

[22] Bancroft, *History of Arizona and New Mexico*, p. 699. See also Darlis Miller, *The California Column in New Mexico* (Albuquerque: University of New Mexico Press, 1982). *J.T.B.*

[23] Adjutant General U.S. Army. Also see Francis B. Heitman, *Historical Register and Dictionary of the United States Army, from its Organization September 29, 1789, to March 2, 1903* (Washington: Government Printing Office, 1903), 1: 649. *J.T.B.*

[24] An excellent exposition on the mines in the Organ Mountains is found in Kingsley C. Duncan, "The Geology of the Organ Mountains," Bulletin #11, State Bureau of Mines and Mineral Resources (Socorro: New Mexico School of Mines, 1935). J.T.B.

[25] *Ibid.*, pp. 228-229. *J.T.B.*

[26] *Ibid.*, pp. 214-219. *J.T.B.*

[27] *Ibid.*, pp. 185-189, 220-228. *J.T.B.*

[28] *Ibid.*, pp. 189, 220-228. *J.T.B.*

[29] *Ibid.*, pp. 231-234. *J.T.B.*

[30] *Ibid.*, pp. 230-231. *J.T.B.*

[31] *Ibid.*, pp. 237-238. *J.T.B.*

[32] Information on local smelters can be found in John C. Neilson, "Communidad: Community Life in a Southwestern Town, Las Cruces, New Mexico, 1880-1890, master's thesis, New Mexico State University, 1988. *J.T.B.*

CHAPTER IV

<u>Sketches of Prominent Pioneers;</u>
<u>with some mysteries and tragedies.</u>

<u>Acknowledgments</u>

PIONEERS

There are many names to come under the head of the pioneer list. The owners of some of these names are still in the land of the living, but only a few; around some of these names cling pleasant thoughts, while others bring a shudder at the fortune that fell to the lot of the person. It will be remembered that in those early unsettled times the man who was sheriff had to be lion-hearted, and held in some awe by even the roughest. He was supreme in his county and the probate judge a close second, for many, many years; so, the mention of these offices means a great deal to the honor of the man.

I will but mention the most prominent men who have played a part in the history of the Mesilla Valley.

The fourteen settlers at Doña Ana, and those connected with ranches earlier than '42 have been given. After Doña Ana was settled, though the valley was an Indian haunted mesquite jungle, people dared to come and that place became well populated.

With Doniphan, December 25th, 1846, came a man who, ever since his return after the war, has figured more prominently than any other in our Valley. Hon. Samuel G. Bean, born September 10th, 1819, at Maysville, Mason County, Kentucky, spared to a ripe old age, resides at Las Cruces with his wife and family. He made his home in La Mesilla, became very wealthy and influential; he has been honored by every place of trust and responsibility, and is, today, an active reader, and a clear minded and accurate thinker. The writer is most grateful to Mr. Bean for his ever kind attention and assistance to her.

A little later came a Frenchman by the name of Francis Fletcher. He came as a sailor to New Orleans, pushed on through Texas to our frontier valley as a hunter. He was an active, intelligent man and was of great service in those early days as interpreter for the officers and settlers. Wealth came to him rapidly; he married a Miss Lucero, bought the wide extending Alameda grounds, and built a large ranch house. The old building, some walls still standing, may be seen on the opposite side of the main acequia beyond what is now called the Alameda Ranch Resort.[1] This Fletcher home was noted for its hospitality and elegance. It was built about 1855. Four children came to the home, only one of whom, Mrs. Guadalupe Ascarate of Las Cruces, is alive. Mr. Fletcher died at his ranch July 15th, 1878.

One of the earliest settlers was Adolph Lea, who has passed away with [in] a few weeks of this writing. Mr. Lea for almost thirty years made his home at Leasburg, a town north of Doña Ana named in honor of his large possessions and prominence. He was a sutler for years at Ft. Selden, and obtained the start to his wealth in this capacity. Mr. Lea was a most intelligent man; his last years were spent teaching his bright little grand-children, the children of Mr. Dan Read, of Las Cruces.

Around the name of John Lemon clings the most awful tragedy in the annals of the Mesilla Valley. In the earliest '60s John Lemon came to La Mesilla from California. He was a Unionist and came perilously near losing his life for his country. Soon the Confederate element prevailed at La Mesilla, and Lemon, together with two friends, Jacob Applezoller and Critenden Marshall, were arrested and imprisoned. At night these three men were taken from the guard house by a company of citizens to a thicket of trees where Marshal was hung until he was dead, Applezoller was treated the same way, though he was cut down before he had expired, and spent the rest of his days peaceably in Texas, but for some reason Lemon was spared. These two were taken back to prison, and later Lemon effected an escape to Ft. Craig. With the retreat of the Confederate army, he came back to his home, and became very wealthy and influential. He was the leader in politics for many years, and was running for office when he met his violent death. August 27th, 1871, was before an election, and it so happened that both sides planned a parade and celebration to take place on the same day; neither side would give in, so both came off. It appears that the two parties met at the south-east corner of the Plaza, near the old church, and melee ensued. It proved that one party was armed and expecting trouble; the other not so. A printer by the name of Kelly started the riot by rushing at Mr. Lemon, the Republican leader, and crushing his skull with a club. As the wounded man fell, he managed to draw his revolver and shot his assassin twice, while friends flew at him also and fairly tore him to pieces. Lemon lived but a few hours.

In the meantime pistol shots flew fast, and in the Plaza were only Democrats; in a few moments, the Republicans rallied armed on the house tops, and not a creature dared show itself on the streets. The justice of the peace came out and commanded order; the tree behind which he leaped was the target for dozens of bullets. Troops were sent for and they alone could maintain order, so infuriated were the Republicans over the murder of their leader. The result of this riot has been given above.[2]

Horace Stephenson was educated in the St. Louis University, and when not at school and until 1859 when he married, he lived at his father's splendid home in Concordia, Texas, just below El Paso. The Hugh Stephenson of whom such frequent mention has been made in connection with the Bracito Grant and mines, never lived in the valley though he was intimately associated with its people and business interests. Horace Stephenson settled permanently in Las Cruces in 1875, and has been one or our most prominent men; he resides today, surrounded by his lovely family, in the well known Stephenson block at Las Cruces.

Hon. Stephen B. Elkins, of the United States Senate, arrived in the Mesilla Valley in the early part of 1865. During his first years in Doña Ana County, Senator Elkins became interested in local questions and was sent to the Legislature in Santa Fé; he afterwards practiced law, and spent his first money purchasing the library belonging to Judge Knapp. Not very much later, he moved away and has made his name and successful career in wider circles than the Mesilla Valley, where he made his start in politics.

Nestor Armijo who lives in his fine old home in Las Cruces, was a New Mexican, his home being at Albuquerque. At one time Mr. Armijo owned a large store in what is now called the Freudenthal Block; he owns much property in the valley. Mr. and Mrs. Armijo came in the latter part of the '50s; and Mr. Armijo has massed his fortune here almost entirely.

Hon. Thomas B. Catron, now and for years back one of the most prominent political leaders of our territory, was born October 6th, 1840, in Lafayette County, Missouri. He came to New Mexico in 1866, and located at La Mesilla February 22nd, 1867, commencing the practice of law there. The next year he was sent to the legislature, and then took up his resident in Santa Fé where he has lived since. Mr. Catron met the charming lady he married at La Mesilla. He has been our delegate at Washington, and is very wealthy.

Don Barbaro Lucero came to the Mesilla Valley when a young man and held an important position on the famous boundary survey in its varied career. Mr. Lucero resides in Las Cruces; among his other property he owns the Lucero mill in the north of town. His two children have married and settled here, and are together with their father, our most respected citizens.

Rebellion fortunes brought many settlers, among whom Col. A[lbert] J. Fountain, Major Eugene Van Patten, Col. W[illiam] L. Rynerson, John Martin, John Barncastle, and many, many more, as California Volunteers.[3] After an honorable and useful life here, occupying government positions, and taking an active part in politics, Col. A.J. Fountain was suddenly taken from his devoted wife and family. Around the event is a complete shadow, and is one of the many mysteries that will be revealed sometime. Col. Fountain and [his] seven year old boy, Henry, were crossing the vast plains on the east side of the Organs from court in Lincoln, in 1895. The gentleman was United States prosecuting attorney, and at that term of court had attempted to run down some notorious cattle thieves. He was in possession of valuable papers, when he started home across the plains in his buckboard, for it happened he was delayed, so missed going with other officials—but he cheerily called to the stage driver who urged him to go with the stage that he was not afraid. Neither he nor his child have ever been seen nor heard of since. It is supposed that he was ridden down by cattle thieves, murdered, and all traces so cleverly obliterated, that, though the most careful search has been made by enraged and sorrow-stricken friends, no clues as to the fate of the poor father and son, or murderers, have been held. Col. Fountain left a large family, the members of which reside in the valley and are respected citizens.

The name of Hon. Eugene Van Patten is familiar and loved by us all. 'Major Van' came to the valley early, and has played an active part in politics and business life ever since he came. In the early days he was sheriff, and the full significance of that important office is known. Hon. Van Patten owned a large hotel which was known far and wide, with much other property. He lost his wife many, many years ago, and his one child, a daughter, married into one of our prominent families, her name being Mrs. James Ascarate.

Major Van Patten when not traveling over the territory on military affairs is to be found at his beautiful, well known mountain resort, Van Patten's Dripping Springs.

Col. W.L. Rynerson, who we, as children remember as the '<u>very tallest</u>' of men, was a very wealthy, valuable citizen. He married, in the early '70s, Mrs. J[ohn] Lemon, at La Mesilla; and, at his death a few years ago, just after completing a beautiful large house in Las Cruces, his children divided a large estate.

John Martin, born in Caledonia, New York, went through the Mexican War, then left the army and went to California. August, 1861, he was appointed 1st Lieut. of Company D, 1st California Infantry, and with his troops was sent to the Rio Grande Valley. In Arizona, his captain died, and Mr. Martin assumed command; he was discharged in '64, married the next year at Las Cruces, and settled at Fort Selden where he ran the ferry boat for some time. In 1869 he struck water on the fearful desert 'Jornada del Muerto,' and thereby relieved the journey south of much of its horror, and ever after that was called 'Jack Martin, the Chief of the Jornada.' His death occurred March 9th, 1877, in Santa Fé, where he owned the leading hotel. Not one of the Martin family reside in the valley.

The name of Ochoa is much mixed in the history of our valley. Four penniless brothers sought their fortune at Doña Ana, very early in the pioneer days. One brother, Guadalupe Ochoa, was drowned while attempting to cross from Las Cruces to La Mesilla. One spring in the early '60s the waters were raging, but business was urgent, so he got in the boat, and grasping the rope which was stretched across the river, endeavored to make his way. The water was irresistible, the boat was swept from beneath him, and the unfortunate man was drowned. The three others are living today in Mexico and Arizona, and are millionaires.

Thomas J. Bull came from Ohio in 1851 or 1852, and established himself in the mercantile business in the Duper block which is almost all torn down now. In 1855 he moved to La Mesilla. Mr. Bull accumulated a vast amount of riches, and at one time was the wealthiest and most influential man in the Mesilla Valley. Mr. Bull died about three years ago; his descendants are engaged in the grandfather's vocation at La Mesilla.

Rafael Ruelas, an original settler of La Mesilla, passed away many years ago. He was an official under the Mexican government, and was a most respected citizen.

Another of the very earliest men of La Mesilla was Eugenio Moreno who came from Canton Jaleana, Mexico. Besides being one of our early representatives to the legislature, he served his government in other capacities. Mr. Moreno went first to Doña Ana, then to La Mesilla, finally moving to La Mesa in 1860 where he remained until his death about six years ago. Sons of the gentleman are in the valley in commercial life today.

In connection with Moreno and Ruelas should be mentioned other pioneers, such as Joseph F. Bennett, the Ascarate Brothers, and Mr. [Alfred J.] Buchoz. Mr. Buchoz was of French descent; but was Americanized and went from Michigan to Juárez as a clerk. In 1855 or 1856, he went to La Mesilla, and became a valuable citizen. His family of boys have scattered from the valley and are now in business. Mr. Buchez has been dead many years.

Henry J. Cuniffe came to the valley from Mexico in 1847; he married a Miss Lujan of Las Cruces, who still survives him. Mr. Cuniffe, at different times during his life, was probate judge, sheriff, assessor, and served as United States Consul at Juárez, Mexico, while it was the capital of the Mexican Republic, under President Benito Juárez, who was driven north by Maximilian.

Don Pedro Aguirre came to the Mesilla Valley from Chihuahua in 1852 and settled on a ranch between Doña Ana and Las Cruces. His family claims that he brought the first coffee to these parts; also, the first wagon that had any iron about it or spokes to the wheels. Formerly people used what were called 'carretas'—vehicles of wood with even, huge solid wheels which creaked and groaned so loudly that they could be heard for almost incredible distance; this noise was very humorously described in the Marvelous Country by Cozzens.[4]

Of Numa Reymond and Don Pablo Melendrez I have spoken before in previous pages, so will not here.

Daniel Frietze was one of the original settlers of La Mesilla. He came from El Paso del Norte where he was a clerk for Miranda. He came to own much property in the valley; he held various positions, and was a very popular man. Mr. Frietze lived continuously in La Mesilla until his death, six or seven years ago.

Louis Flote was a French-American who lived and died in Las Cruces in the very early days. Through a wealthy marriage he got possession of the celebrated Coralitas mines in Mexico, and he was also interested in the early Stephenson mine. He owned a large store in what is now called the Lane block, in the early '50s. When with a freight train on the river, nearly opposite San Marcial, in the year 1855, he received a bruise on the knee, but, thinking it slight, paid no attention to it. Not many months later the wound caused his death; the surgeons at Ft. Fillmore performed two amputations, and every care was taken, his life could not be saved.

The name of May is most familiar. The father of our energetic businessmen came from Germany to St. Louis, on to Santa Fé, and finally started up in business in Las Cruces in 1851. Mrs. May arrived in 1854; and in the territory were born all the six children that make up this popular family. Hotel business was Mr. [John L.] May's line, and the house was known all over the Southwest. Mr. May passed away only a few years ago.

Probably the saddest story of all, is that to be told about Isidor Armijo, one of the very earliest residents of Las Cruces. Mr. Armijo came from Socorro, and made his home in the large house that today goes by his name. The family of this gentleman consisted of his wife and twelve sons; he was interested in the famous Gran Quivere mines, and, when on a trip to them with eleven of his sons, they were attacked and all killed by the Indians. This was over thirty years ago. The twelfth son, Jacinto Armijo, had remained in Las Cruces and so escaped being murdered. He grew to manhood, raised a family, and had a tragic death a few years ago.

Samuel J. Jones came, in 1858, to La Mesilla, in the capacity of Collector of Customs for El Paso del Norte, with the privilege of living at Las Cruces. That same year he became sutler at Ft. Fillmore; he gave up the Collectorship in 1861, and when the troops left Ft. Fillmore he moved to La Mesilla. The next year he was deputy revenue collector; a few years later he became clerk of the district court, and in 1884, after having been almost helpless for many years, he passed away.

A son of Col. Samuel J. Jones, William T. Jones, was a practicing lawyer and was our representative in the House in 1876-7. His death, which occurred in 1879, while he was serving his second term as Probate Clerk of Doña Ana County, was a very sad one. William Jones, with seventeen other volunteers, was killed in a affair with about seventy-five Apache Indians, fifteen miles northeast of the old Slocum ranch.

Hon. Mariano Barela passed away in La Mesilla many years ago. He was an early settler, and one of the most prominent and wealthiest in the valley during the '70s. Besides being sheriff for two terms, he occupied at his death an important government position. His widow is alive still, and resides in the big old Barela homestead just outside of La Mesilla.

Richard Campbell went to Santa Fé in the early '40s, married into a prominent Mexican family, and served as sheriff there for two terms. He then moved to Las Cruces as one of its few, and was the first probate judge, serving three terms.

In 1858, becoming enthusiastic over the reports of fabulous gold deposits and the Gila river—Gila country was then in Doña Ana County—he, with his youngest son, a youth of 15, made his way over there. The old man soon sickened and died, and the son, after burying his father, made his way back to Las Cruces. Mr. Campbell left his large family in moderate circumstances; he was a most popular old man, and one of strict integrity, as declared by all the friends who now survive him.

Notes:

[1] Located on current day Townsend Terrace. *J.T.B.*

[2] See also Mills, *Forty Years at El Paso*, pp. 71-72; George W. Griggs, *History of Mesilla Valley or The Gadsden Purchase* (Mesilla: n.p., 1930), 90-93. *J.T.B.*

[3] For more on the California Volunteers who settled in the Mesilla Valley see Miller, *The California Column in New Mexico. J.T.B.*

[4] Cozzens, *The Marvelous Country*, p. 58.

ACKNOWLEDGMENTS

The writer has felt free to consult available and reliable literature on matters relative to the history contained in this work. She wishes to express her grateful acknowledgment for the interest and encouragement received from citizens of the Mesilla Valley, and those in various parts of the country who have so generously aided her in searching for data.

Thanks are due particularly to the following gentlemen who have given so readily and willingly to the material used in the writing of this thesis:

Hon. Samuel G. Bean	Las Cruces, N.M.
Hon. Horace Stephenson	" "
Hon. Adolph Lea	" "
Hon. W.W. Mills	U.S. Consul, Chihuahua, Mexico
Sen. Stephen B. Elkins	U.S. Senate, Washington, D.C.
Hon. Numa Reymond	25 Quai du Leman, Geneve, Suisse (Switzerland)
Don Nestor Armijo	Las Cruces, N.M.
Don Barbaro Lucero	" "

INDEX